FOURTH EDITION

READY TO WRITE 1

A FIRST COMPOSITION TEXT

KAREN BLANCHARD • CHRISTINE ROOT

We dedicate this book to Evelyn Rose Blanchard, Owen Baker Root, Parker Allen Root, and August James Root, the newest members of our team.

Ready to Write 1: A First Composition Text
Fourth Edition

Pearson Education, 221 River Street, Hoboken, NJ 07030

Acknowledgments: We are grateful to Jeff Diluglio, John Dumicich, Carolyn Graham, Jane Sloan, and Robby Steinberg for helping us keep the purpose of this text in focus.

Staff credits: The people who made up the *Ready to Write* team, representing editorial, production, design, and manufacturing, are Pietro Alongi, Tracey Cataldo, Rosa Chapinal, Aerin Csigay, Mindy DePalma, Warren Fischbach, Pam Fishman, Leslie Johnson, Niki Lee, Amy McCormick, Robert Ruvo, and Kristina Skof.
Development Editor: Penny Laporte
Cover image: Evgeny Karandaev / Shutterstock
Text composition: ElectraGraphics, Inc.
Text font: Formata Light
Photo credits: p1BL: Smuki/Fotolia; p1BR: Alexkich/Fotolia; p1CR: Oocoskun/Fotolia; p1TL: Luismolinero/Fotolia; p1TR: Razihusin/Fotolia; p8: Rob/Fotolia; p12: Vadymvdrobot/Fotolia; p14: Aastock/Shutterstock; p16BC: Jovannig/Fotolia; p16BCL: Gareth Boden/Pearson Education, Inc.; p16BCR: Iko/Shutterstock; p16BL: Freeskyline/Fotolia; p16BR: Michaeljung/Fotolia; p16C: Michaelcourtney/Fotolia; p16CB: Gstockstudio/Fotolia; p16CBL: AlenD/Fotolia; p16CBR: MaxFrost/Fotolia; p16CL: Kurhan/Fotolia; p16CML: BillionPhotos/Fotolia; p16CMR: Gstockstudio/Fotolia; p16CR: Iconogenic/Fotolia; p16MT: Zdenka Darula/Fotolia; p16TCL: Michaeljung/Fotolia; p16TCR: Kite Rin/Fotolia; p16TL: Imagesetc/Fotolia; p16TR: Rido/Fotolia; p44: Baibaz/Fotolia; p49BC: Pikselstock/Fotolia; p49BL: Eugenesergeev/Fotolia; p49BR: Konstantin Sutyagin/Shutterstock; p49TC: Inesbazdar/Fotolia; p49TL: Elnariz/Fotolia; p49TR: Lisa F. Young/Fotolia; p50: Valeriy Velikov/Fotolia; p61: © Randy Glasbergen/glasbergen.com; p69: Horten/Fotolia; p74: © Randy Glasbergen/glasbergen.com; p75: Val Thoermer/Shutterstock; p87: Puwanai/Shutterstock; p107BC: PhotoKD/Fotolia; p107BL: Creative_stock/Fotolia; p107BR: Petr Malyshev/Fotolia; p107C: DC Studio/Fotolia; p107CR: karagrubis/Fotolia; p113L: Mikhail Bakunovich/Shutterstock; p113R: Algre/Fotolia; p128: Bettmann/Corbis; p129: Iriana Shiyan/Fotolia; p140: Dpa picture alliance/Alamy Stock Photo; p147: Kichigin19/Fotolia; p148: Universal Images Group North America LLC/Alamy Stock Photo; p151: Presselect/Alamy Stock Photo; p153: PCN Photography/Alamy Stock Photo; p155B: ZUMA Press, Inc./Alamy Stock Photo; p155T: Marka/Alamy Stock Photo; p159: Marchello74/123RF; p161BC: Igor Mojzes/Fotolia; p161BL: Monkey Business Images/Shutterstock; p161BR: Starflamedia/Fotolia; p161TC: Badahos/Fotolia; p161TL: Manfred Steinbach/123RF; p161TR: MnyJhee/Fotolia; p162BC: Pavel Losevsky/Fotolia; p162BL: Andris Piebalgs/Fotolia; p162BR: Gemenacom/Fotolia; p162TCL: Jules Selmes/Pearson Education, Inc.; p162TCR: Syda Productions/Fotolia; p162TL: Rilueda/Fotolia; p162TR: Dangubic/Fotolia; p165L: Studio7192/Fotolia; p165R: Africa Studio/Fotolia; p166BL: Jinga80/Fotolia; p166BR: Pathdoc/Fotolia; p166TL: Rob Marmion/Shutterstock; p166TR: Vadymvdrobot/Fotolia; p172: Robert Kneschke/Shutterstock; p173C: Somchai Som/Shutterstock; p173L: James Steidl/Shutterstock; p173R: Montree104/Fotolia; p174BC: Douglas Tomko/Fotolia; p174BL: James Steidl/Shutterstock; p174BR: Victor Shova/Shutterstock; p174TC: Grebcha/Shutterstock; p174TL: Marc Dietrich/Shutterstock; p174TR: Arogant/Shutterstock

Library of Congress Cataloging-in-Publication Data
A catalog record for the print edition is available from the Library of Congress.
ISBN-10: 0-13-440065-8   ISBN-13: 978-0-13-440065-5

Printed in the United States of America
4   17

Contents

Scope and Sequence

Chapter	Grammar for Writing	Paragraph Pointers	Writing Activities	Real-life Writing
1 **WRITING ABOUT YOURSELF** **Learning Outcomes:** Write a paragraph about yourself or someone you know Complete a student information form	Capital letters	Simple sentences Paragraph form	Using the writing process Writing about yourself Writing a about your classmate **WORD BANKS** **Learning words about:** Languages Jobs	Filling out a form
2 **WRITING ABOUT YOUR FAMILY AND FRIENDS** **Learning Outcomes:** Write a paragraph introducing your family or friend Write an email to a friend	Subject and object pronouns Possessive adjectives Compound sentences with *and, but*	Titles	Using the writing process Writing about your family Writing about a friend Writing a paragraph about your future family **WORD BANK** **Learning words about:** Family	Writing an email to family and friends
3 **WRITING ABOUT YOUR ACTIVITIES** **Learning Outcomes:** Write a paragraph about your free-time activities Write an email inviting a friend to do something with you	Simple present tense: statements, *yes / no* questions, *wh-* questions	Paragraph structure	Using the writing process Writing about free-time activities Writing about staying healthy **WORD BANKS** **Learning words about:** Daily activities Free-time activities Healthy habits	Writing an email inviting a friend to join you in activities

Chapter	Grammar for Writing	Paragraph Pointers	Writing Activities	Real-life Writing
4 **GIVING INSTRUCTIONS** **Learning Outcomes:** Write a paragraph about how to make or do something Write a recipe card	Count nouns and noncount nouns Imperative Sentences	Time-order signal words Time Order Paragraphs	Using the writing process Writing about how to make or do something **WORD BANK** **Learning words about:** Cooking	Writing a recipe card
5 **WRITING ABOUT YOUR DAY** **Learning Outcomes:** Write a paragraph about a special or typical day Write a message on a greeting card	Prepositions of time Frequency adverbs Combining sentences with *before* and *after*	Time-order paragraphs Paragraph unity	Using the writing process Writing about someone's typical day or special days **WORD BANKS** **Learning words about:** Frequency Time-order Weekday activities	Writing a greeting card
6 **WRITING DESCRIPTIONS** **Learning Outcomes:** Write a descriptive paragraph about a person or thing Complete an order form, and write a lost and found message	Present progressive: statements, *yes / no* questions, *wh-* questions Adjectives	Examples to support topic sentences Details to support sentences	Using the writing process Writing descriptive paragraphs about yourself and people you know Writing descriptive paragraphs about things you have, items you want, products from your country **WORD BANKS** **Learning words about:** Physical characteristics Clothes and personal items Opinions (adjectives) Personality Cars	Completing an order form Writing lost-and-found messages

Chapter	Grammar for Writing	Paragraph Pointers	Writing Activities	Real-life Writing
7 **WRITING ABOUT PLACES** **Learning Outcomes:** Write a paragraph describing a place Write a friendly letter and address an envelope	*There is / There are* Prepositions of place	Space-order paragraphs	Using the writing process Describing rooms Describing a picture **WORD BANKS** **Learning words about:** Rooms Descriptions (adjectives) Prepositions of place	Writing a friendly letter Addressing an envelope
8 **WRITING A NARRATIVE** **Learning Outcomes:** Write a paragraph about an experience Write a postcard about a vacation	Simple past tense: statements, *yes / no* questions, *wh-* questions	Narrative paragraphs	Using the writing process Writing about a personal experience Writing about an experience in a traffic jam Writing a biography Writing an autobiography Writing poetry about special memories	Writing a postcard
9 **EXPRESSING YOUR OPINION** **Learning Outcomes:** Write an opinion paragraph Write a letter to the editor	*Should* for opinions and advice with	Order of importance paragraphs	Using the writing process Writing an opinion about different topics Writing letters asking for and giving advice **WORD BANKS** **Learning words about:** Public places Order of importance (signal words) Inventions	Writing a letter to the editor

Introduction

Ready to Write 1 is a beginning level writing skills textbook for English language students who have some limited knowledge of both written and spoken English. It is a text designed to acquaint students with the basic skills required for good writing, and to help them become comfortable, confident, and independent writers in English.

The *Ready to Write* series came about because of our threefold conviction that

- students learn to write well and achieve a more complete English proficiency by learning and practicing writing skills simultaneously with other English language skills they are learning;

- students are interested in and capable of writing expressively in English—however simple the language—on a variety of provocative and sophisticated topics if they are supplied with the basic vocabulary and organizational tools;

- students need to be explicitly taught that different languages organize information differently, and they need to be shown how to organize information correctly in English.

Approach

Although it is a writing text, *Ready to Write 1* integrates reading, speaking, and listening skills with prewriting, writing, and revising. As in *Ready to Write 2* and *Ready to Write 3,* students are called upon to write frequently and on a broad range of topics. *Ready to Write 1* is based on the premise that students, even at this level, can and want to express themselves in English. What they need in order to do so effectively is an ever-expanding vocabulary base and successive opportunities to write short, confidence-building pieces.

It is our intention in *Ready to Write 1* to introduce, without being overly didactic, the basic skills required for good writing in English. Through an abundance of pair and group activities as well as individual writing tasks, students learn the fundamental principles of the writing process: prewriting, planning, drafting, revising, and editing as they move from sentence-level writing to guided paragraphs and beyond. In addition, given the important link between grammar, vocabulary and good writing, we have made the grammar and vocabulary practice more obvious, expanded the explanations, and added more practice opportunities.

The Fourth Edition

While much has been updated and expanded in this Fourth Edition of *Ready to Write 1,* what has not changed is the successful, basic approach that has made the series so popular all these years.

Popular features from previous editions have been expanded and appear regularly in this new edition. *You Be the Editor* focuses on the specific grammar point studied in each chapter. *Word Banks* have been enlarged to supply students with additional useful, pertinent vocabulary. *On Your Own* and *Use Your Imagination* provide students with further, less structured writing practice. Students are encouraged to assemble a portfolio of their work comprising the paragraphs, letters, poems, and drawings that they produce throughout the course.

The fourth edition of *Ready to Write 1* includes these important new and expanded features:

- learning outcomes at the beginning of each chapter to focus students on the chapter's goals
- an engaging four-color design to help learners' visual literacy and highlight key features
- updated and reinforced explanations and model paragraphs
- extensive, targeted grammar practice to help students become effective writers
- extended word banks to increase topic-based vocabulary
- enhanced and increased sentence and paragraph writing tasks to encourage experimentation and bolster writing practice and accuracy
- *Essential Online Resources* with answer keys, as well as additional grammar and writing activities.

Chapter Features

Learning Outcomes: Each chapter begins with objectives so students can see the intended goals of a chapter and what their learning experience will be. The learning outcomes are brief, written statements that help students see the knowledge, skills, and habits of work that they are expected to acquire by the end of the chapter. There are two learning outcomes: one for paragraph writing and one for life skills writing.

Word Banks: The expanded word banks introduce topic related vocabulary the students can exploit as they read, talk and write about the topic. In many cases, exercises allow students to practice identifying, using, forming, and expanding on this vocabulary. The boxes are clearly identified and the vocabulary sets defined.

Grammar for Writing: Each chapter focuses on one or two specific grammar points along with helpful charts, clear explanations, and attendant practice. By practicing new grammar points in the context of their writing, students boost their writing accuracy and learn to vary their sentence types.

Paragraph Pointers: This feature provides information on how to write unified, coherent, and well-developed paragraphs. Students learn about the basic structure of an English paragraph i.e. topic, supporting and concluding sentences. Among others, they also learn about the importance of including signal words, examples, and details in their writing.

The Steps of the Writing Process: Each chapter provides guided instruction in the steps that are integral to good writing i.e. prewriting, writing, and revising. Revising checklists are provided for students to use to improve their paragraphs and write their final draft.

On Your Own: Coming toward the end of most chapters, these activities provide students with yet another opportunity to write on a topic of their own choosing from among several suggested prompts. After they write a paragraph, students are instructed to use the revising checklist to improve their paragraphs, thereby practicing independent writing and revising.

You Be the Editor: This self-correcting exercise near the end of each chapter is intended to give students the opportunity to look for and correct the most common grammar mistakes made by high beginning students as they learn to write in English. Each paragraph has a stated number of mistakes for students to look for. The answers for each chapter appear in the back of the book. Students can use the answers to check their own work and become become independent and confident learners.

Real Life Writing: Each chapter concludes with an example of the kinds of writing people commonly do in their day-to-day lives. These real-world writing tasks include completing forms, writing email and letters, and addressing envelopes.

We hope that you and your students enjoy the activities in this text. No matter their level, they are *ready to write.*
—KLB and CBR

CHAPTER 1 ‣ Writing about Yourself

LEARNING OUTCOMES

Paragraph Writing: Write a paragraph about yourself or someone you know
Real-Life Writing: Complete a student information form

Learning to write in a new language is not always easy, but it can be fun. If you are learning to speak and read in a new language, you are ready to begin writing, too. The exercises in this book will help you become a better writer in English.

The easiest way to begin writing is to write about things you know well. That often means writing about yourself. You will find it interesting and helpful to keep your writing in a special folder called a portfolio.

INTRODUCING YOURSELF

A Look at the cover that a student designed for his portfolio.

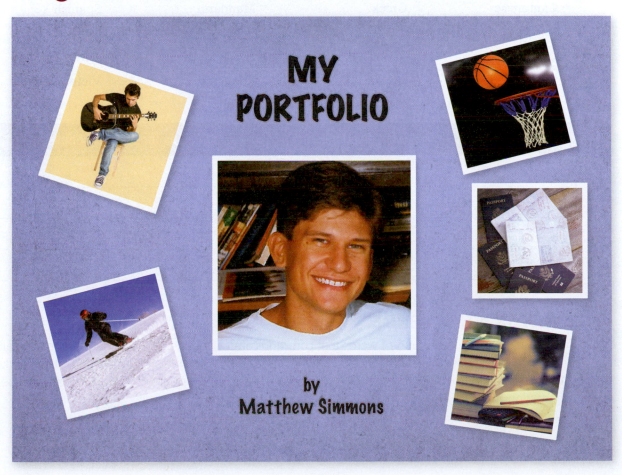

1

B Design the cover for your portfolio on a separate piece of paper. Use drawings, photos, words, or print out images from the Internet to describe who you are. Here are some suggestions for things to include:

- your family and friends
- your interests and favorite activities
- sports you like to play or watch
- your job, profession, or major in school
- your favorite places, foods, holidays, activities

C Share the cover of your portfolio with your classmates.

D Write your name on the board and teach your classmates how to pronounce it. Does your name have a special meaning in your language? What does it mean?

E Work in small groups. Tell the people in your group what language(s) you speak. Use the word bank to help you with spelling. Also tell your group why you are studying English. Then complete the chart with the correct information.

LANGUAGES WORD BANK

Throughout this book, you will see many Word Banks. These Word Banks include useful words for your writing. Improving your vocabulary is an important part of improving your writing. Using the new words you learn will make your writing better and more interesting.

Arabic	German	Korean	Russian
Cantonese	Greek	Mandarin	Spanish
Czech	Indonesian	Polish	Thai
Dutch	Italian	Portuguese	Turkish
French	Japanese	Romanian	Vietnamese

Name	Languages	Reasons for Studying English

WHAT IS A SENTENCE?

An English sentence is a group of words that communicates a complete thought. All sentences start with a capital letter and most sentences end with a period (.). Questions end with a question mark (?). An exclamation point (!) shows strong feeling, such as surprise or anger. We usually do not use exclamation marks in formal writing.

GRAMMAR FOR WRITING: Simple Sentences

A simple sentence may be long or short, but all sentences must have a **subject** and a **verb**. Many sentences have an **object** or a **complement**, too. The order of words in a sentence is important. The most common order for English sentences is *subject + verb + object* (or *complement*).

Study the chart below to learn about the parts of a simple sentence.

Part of Sentence	Explanation
subject **Seong** speaks Korean. subject **He** plays soccer.	**SUBJECT** The **subject** is a person or thing that does the action. It is usually a noun or a pronoun. The subject comes at the beginning of a sentence before the verb.
verb Marsha **drives** her car to work every day. verb She **sings** in a band.	**VERB** The **verb** usually describes the action. It comes after the subject. The verb may be one word or more than one word.
object Steve studied **Cantonese** in college. object My mother is baking **a cake**.	**OBJECT** Most verbs (such as *play, read, give, speak*) describe an action. The **object** is the person or thing that receives the action. The object usually answers the question *What?* or *Who(m)?*
subject linking verb complement Izumi is **Japanese**. subject linking verb complement Paulo was **a teacher**.	**COMPLEMENT** Some verbs, called linking verbs, do not describe an action. A linking verb connects the subject of the sentence to information about the subject. The most common linking verb in English is *be*. In sentences with linking verbs, the verb is followed by an adjective or noun, called a **complement**, which describes something about the subject of a sentence.

PRACTICE Circle the verb in each sentence. Underline the subject. Draw a box around the object or complement.

1. Mr. Robertson is Australian.

2. Chris kicked the soccer ball.

3. She is shy.

4. Andrea and Marshall ride bikes.

5. He is a banker.

6. We are watching a movie.

7. They are funny.

8. Leo drives a taxi.

9. Mr. Yang is painting a picture.

10. The teacher corrects our exams.

11. Mario is friendly.

12. Aiko and Julie are nervous.

DESCRIBING WHAT YOU DO

The question *What do you do?* has a special meaning in English. It means *What is your job?* We use the verb *be* to answer this question. For example, *I am a mechanic.* If you are in school, you can say, *I am a student,* or *I'm in nursing school.*

PRACTICE **A** **Read the sentences. They all use a form of the verb *be*. Circle the verb in each sentence.**

1. I am a teacher.

2. You are a student.

3. She is an engineer.

4. He is a waiter.

5. We are salespeople.

6. They are nurses.

7. Kim is a high school student.

8. Ali is a businessman.

9. I am a dental student.

B **Look at the sentences in Exercise A and answer the questions.**

1. Which subject uses *am*?

_____

2. Which subjects use *is*?

_____

3. Which subjects use *are*?

_____

C Study the word bank. Find out what some of your classmates do. Ask "What do you do?" Write sentences about four classmates. Use the correct form of the verb *be*.

JOBS WORD BANK

administrative assistant	hairstylist	photographer
artist	homemaker	plumber
baker	journalist/reporter	police officer
bank teller	judge	receptionist
bus/taxi driver	lawyer	salesperson
businessperson	mail carrier	student
computer programmer	mechanic	veterinarian
cook/chef	medical technician	waiter
customer service representative	nurse	web designer

Example: Rose is a receptionist.

1. _____

2. _____

3. _____

4. _____

D Choose four of your classmates. Talk about their jobs. Ask questions such as, *Where do you work? What do you do in your job?* Write two to three sentences about their jobs.

Example:

Classmate's name: Rose

1. She works in a doctor's office.

2. She answers the phone.

3. She makes appointments.

Classmate's name: _____

1. _____

2. _____

3. _____

Classmate's name: _____

1. _____

2. _____

3. _____

Classmate's name: _____

1. _____

2. _____

3. _____

Classmate's name: _____

1. _____

2. _____

3. _____

GRAMMAR FOR WRITING: Capital Letters

The first word of every sentence begins with a capital letter. Other important words in English begin with a capital letter, too.

Study the rules below for using capital letters.

Rules: Always Capitalize . . .	Examples
1. the first word of every new sentence and question	**H**is name is Matthew Simmons. **W**hat is your name?
2. the pronoun *I*	Harris and **I** like to play tennis together.
3. the names and titles of people	He has a meeting with **D**r. **C**arol **W**olf. I call **S**ong **Y**ee every day.
4. the names of streets, cities, states, countries, continents, stores, and restaurants	The library is on **J**uniper **S**treet. She is from **A**ustin, **T**exas. They live in **L**ima, **P**eru. **P**eru is in **S**outh **A**merica. My favorite restaurant is **D**evon. I buy my groceries at **S**hop **S**mart.

Rules: Always Capitalize . . .	Examples
5. days of the week and months of the year	His birthday is next **T**hursday. We're going on vacation in **J**une.
6. the names of languages and nationalities	He speaks **V**ietnamese. My grandparents are **M**exican.

PRACTICE **Rewrite each sentence. Add the capital letters.**

1. i like to travel.

   _____

2. yumi lives in tokyo, japan.

   _____

3. i am from from mexico.

   _____

4. mr. kim has a meeting on friday.

   _____

5. ali studies spanish and english.

   _____

6. my birthday is in july.

   _____

7. what is your native language?

   _____

8. julio works at the restaurant on friday.

   _____

9. is mrs. kara in the library?

   _____

10. I buy most of my shoes at a new store called hot foot.

    _____

WHAT IS A PARAGRAPH?

Most English writing is organized into paragraphs. You will write many paragraphs in this book. A paragraph is a group of sentences about one main idea. This main idea is called the *topic*.

PARAGRAPH POINTER: Paragraph Form

English paragraphs are written in a special form. Follow these rules when you write a paragraph:

1. Indent the first line of each new paragraph about ½ inch (1.27 centimeters) from the margin.

2. Begin each sentence with a capital letter.

3. End each sentence with correct punctuation. In most sentences this is a period. (Some sentences end in a question mark, or an exclamation point.)

4. The sentences in a paragraph follow each other on the same line. (Do not start each sentence on a new line.)

Read the model paragraph. It is written in the correct form.

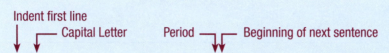

Indent first line
Capital Letter Period Beginning of next sentence

    My name is Matthew Simmons. I am from Boston, Massachusetts. I am twenty-one years old. I speak English and a little Spanish. I am an engineering student at Boston University. I love all kinds of sports. My favorite sports are basketball and skiing. I also like to travel, play guitar, and go to parties with my friends.

PRACTICE **A** **Look at the sentences. Talk with a partner about what is wrong with them.**

my name is Ellen Lang

I am twenty-eight years old

I am from Atlanta, Georgia

my native language is English

I am a chef.

I work at a restaurant called noodles.

of course, i like to cook.

I also like to play the piano and go out with my friends.

B **Write a paragraph using the sentences in Exercise B. Use the correct paragraph form.**

_____

_____

_____

_____

_____

C Add capital letters where necessary. Write a paragraph using these sentences.

1. my name is maggie Costa.

2. i am twenty years old.

3. When i was sixteen, my family moved from new york city to berkeley, california.

4. i did not want to move.

5. I did not want to leave my friends.

6. i liked my school.

7. my teachers were very nice, especially my english teacher, ms. kerner.

8. luckily i liked berkeley right away.

9. we moved in august and by october I was already very happy.

10. my new english teacher, mr. jones, quickly became my new favorite teacher.

11. now I have lived in berkeley for three years.

12. i have made lots of good friends.

13. The weather is great.

14. i never want to leave.

15. it was a good move after all.

A Good Move

_____

_____

_____

_____

_____

_____

_____

_____

_____

THE WRITING PROCESS

Most people cannot write a perfect paragraph on the first try. Each try is called a *draft*. Writing a good paragraph is a process that includes several steps and several drafts. The three main steps are called *prewriting*, *writing*, and *revising*. The exercises in this book will help you practice the steps.

Step 1: Prewriting

Prewriting is anything you do before you write your paragraph. It includes thinking, taking notes, talking to other people, and gathering information.

Step 2: Writing

Writing is putting your ideas into sentences and paragraphs.

Step 3: Revising

Revising is looking for ways to improve your paragraph. When you are revising, you can make corrections and changes to your work.

WRITING A PARAGRAPH ABOUT YOURSELF

Step 1: Prewriting

Look at the cover of your portfolio again. Think about the words and pictures you included. They will help you get ready to write about yourself.

Step 2: Writing

A **Answer these questions about yourself in complete sentences.**

1. What is your complete name?

   _____

2. Where are you from?

   _____

3. Where do you live now?

   _____

4. What language(s) do you speak?

   _____

5. What do you do? (Remember that this question means *What is your job?* The answer begins with *I am a(n)*. For example, you can write, *I am a businessperson*, or *I am a homemaker*.)

_____

6. What do you do in your free time? (For example, do you like to go to the movies? Do you like to play video games? The answer begins with *In my free time, I like to*. For example, you can write, *In my free time, I like to surf the Internet*.)

_____

7. What else do you like to do?

_____

B Use the sentences you wrote to complete a paragraph about yourself. Be sure to follow the rules of paragraph writing.

My name is _____

_____

_____

_____

_____

_____

_____

_____

Step 3: Revising

A Exchange paragraphs with a partner. Read the paragraph your partner wrote. Then use the Revising Checklist to help your partner improve his or her paragraph.

REVISING CHECKLIST	YES	NO
1. Is the first word of the paragraph indented?		
2. Does each sentence begin with a capital letter?		
3. Does each sentence end with a period?		
4. Does each new sentence begin next to the one before it?		

B Use your partner's suggestions and your own ideas to revise your paragraph on a separate piece of paper. Give it the title "About Me" and put it in your portfolio.

WRITING A PARAGRAPH ABOUT A CLASSMATE

💡 **Step 1: Prewriting**

Ⓐ **Work with a partner. Ask and answer these questions. Take notes about your partner's answers.**

1. What is your name?

   _____

2. Do you have children?

   _____

3. Where are you from?

   _____

4. What is your native language?

   _____

5. What do you do?

   _____

6. What do you do in your free time?

   _____

Ⓑ **What else do you want to know about your partner? Ask your partner two more questions and write the answers.**

1. _____

2. _____

🖋 **Step 2: Writing**

Ⓐ **Use the answers from the prewriting step to write complete sentences about your classmate.**

Example:

   My classmate's name is Oscar Alvarez. _____

1. _____

2. _____

3. _____

4. _____

5. _____

6. _____

7. _____

8. _____

B   **Use your sentences to write a paragraph about your classmate. Remember to follow the rules of paragraph writing.**

My classmate's name is _____

_____

_____

_____

_____

_____

_____

_____

_____

_____

_____

Step 3: Revising

A   **Exchange paragraphs with a partner. Read the paragraph your partner wrote. Make sure the information about you is correct. Then use the Revising Checklist to help your partner improve the paragraph.**

REVISING CHECKLIST	YES	NO
1. Is the first word of the paragraph indented?		
2. Does each sentence begin with a capital letter?		
3. Does each sentence end with a period?		
4. Does each new sentence begin next to the one before it?		
5. Are all of the sentences your partner wrote about you correct?		

B   **Use your partner's suggestions to revise your paragraph on a separate piece of paper. Give it the title "My Classmate." Put it in your portfolio.**

ON YOUR OWN

Choose one of the following topics. Follow the three steps (*prewriting, writing,* and *revising*) for writing a paragraph. You can review the three steps on page 10.

- Write a paragraph about your teacher or another one of your classmates. Use the Prewriting questions on page 12 to help you get started.
- Write a paragraph about someone else at your school or workplace.
- Talk to one of your neighbors or roommates. Write a paragraph about him or her.
- Think of someone you like or admire, such as a movie star, sports hero, or politician. Look on the Internet for information that will help you write a paragraph about that person.

YOU BE THE EDITOR

The paragraph "A Lucky and Happy Man" has eight mistakes with capital letters. With a partner, find and correct the mistakes.

A Lucky and Happy Man

My name is Stanley stoico. I am ninety years old. I am from italy. I moved to San Diego, california, with my family when I was nine years old. I speak italian and english. in my younger years, I had many different jobs. I worked hard and saved my money. In 1985, I started my own business. the business was successful, and i retired in 2008. I like to travel and play golf. I have seen and done a lot in my long life. I am a lucky and happy man.

REAL-LIFE WRITING: Filling Out a Form

Fill out the form below with information about yourself.

STUDENT INFORMATION FORM

Please print.

1. Name: _____
                     Last   First   Middle

2. Address: _____

3. Home phone number: _____ Cell phone number: _____

4. Email: _____

5. Gender: _____ M _____ F   Birthday _____ / _____ / _____
                                     month   day   year

6. Marital Status: _____ Single _____ Married _____ Divorced _____ Widowed

7. Nationality: _____

8. First Language: _____

9. Other Languages: _____

10. How long have you studied English?

    _____ Never   _____ 1–2 years

    _____ Less than 1 year   _____ More than 2 years

11. Do you work? _____ Yes _____ No

12. If yes, where? _____ What days and hours? _____

13. Emergency contact (name): _____

    Relationship: _____ Phone number: _____

14. Signature: _____

Writing about Your Family and Friends

LEARNING OUTCOMES

Paragraph Writing: Write a paragraph introducing your family or friend
Real-Life Writing: Write an email to a friend

WRITING ABOUT FAMILY

A Look at Matthew Simmons's family tree. Then ask and answer the questions with a partner. Use words from the word bank on the next page to help you.

Fred Simmons — Harriet Simmons   Stuart Rubin — Tammy Rubin

Martina Geller Simmons — Alan Simmons   Sam Simmons — Evelyn Rubin Simmons   Connie Rubin Berger — Steve Berger

Don Strait — Beth Simmons Strait   Matthew Simmons   Greg Simmons

Chris Simmons   Melissa Simmons   Owen Strait   Andrea Berger   Edward Berger

FAMILY WORD BANK

aunt	granddaughter	nephew	son
brother	grandfather	niece	spouse
child/children	grandmother	parents	stepfather/stepmother
cousin	grandson	relative	stepsister/stepbrother
daughter	husband	sibling	uncle
father	mother	sister	wife

1. Who are Matthew's parents? _____

2. Who are Matthew's uncles? _____

3. Who are Matthew's aunts? _____

4. Who is Matthew's brother? _____

5. Who are Matthew's cousins? _____

6. Who are Matthew's grandmothers? _____

7. Who is Matthew's nephew? _____

B **Complete the chart with words from the word bank.**

Male	Female	Male or Female
uncle		

C **On a separate piece of paper, draw your own family tree. Put it in your portfolio.**

D **Read the model paragraph Matthew Simmons wrote about his family.**

My Family

I have a big family, and we all get along very well. My parents' names are Sam and Evelyn. My mother is a teacher, and my father is an engineer. I have one younger brother. His name is Greg. He is seventeen years old. I also have an older sister named Beth. She is twenty-eight years old, and she works at a bank. She is married to Don Strait. They have a baby boy named Owen. I also have four cousins who live in Boston. My mother's parents live in San Diego, but my father's parents live in Boston. They love to invite the whole family to their house for dinner. Whenever my family gets together, we have a great time.

PARAGRAPH POINTER: Titles

Many paragraphs have a *title.* The title of a paragraph tells the main idea in a few words. Here are some things to remember when you write titles:

- Titles are not complete sentences.
- Always capitalize the first and last words of a title.
- Capitalize all other important words including nouns, verbs, and adjectives. Do not capitalize articles (*a, an, the*) or prepositions (for example *to, from, at, with*)
- Do not use a period at the end of a title. Do not use quotation marks (" ") around the title. But you may use a question mark (?) or an exclamation mark (!).
- Center the title over the paragraph.
- Skip one line between the title and the beginning of the paragraph.

PRACTICE **Correct the titles.**

1. my Favorite hobby _____

2. OUR NEW NEIGHBOR. _____

3. "Free-time is Fun-time" _____

4. Spending Time With Friends _____

5. Fun In The Sun. _____

6. my new baby sister. _____

7. "A Busy Weekend" _____

8. my BEST friend _____

9. a Day At the Zoo _____

10. Learning TO knit Is Easy _____

GRAMMAR FOR WRITING: Pronouns

A **pronoun** is a word that replaces a noun. Pronouns are useful in writing. They help you connect sentences without repeating the same nouns. Two of the most common kinds of pronouns are **subject pronouns** and **object pronouns**.

Subject Pronouns

Subject pronouns (such as *we, she, they*) can be the subject of a sentence. You can use a subject pronoun when the noun it is replacing has already been mentioned. Do not repeat the noun when you use a pronoun in a sentence.

Correct: *Samantha is an English teacher.* **She** *works at a small private school.*

Incorrect: *Samantha is an English teacher. Samantha* **she** *works at a small private school.*

Study the chart. Notice that pronouns can be singular or plural.

Singular Subject Pronouns	Examples	Plural Subject Pronouns	Examples
I	**I** speak Arabic and English.	we	**We** have a new house.
you	**You** have a beautiful daughter.	you	**You** are my best friend.
he, she, it	SUBJECT (Debbie) is my sister. **She** is eighteen years old. (She = Debbie) SUBJECT (Abdullah) is my cousin. **He** works at a bank. (He = Abdullah) SUBJECT (The movie) was great. **It** was scary. (It = the movie)	they	**They** have lots of cousins.

 A **Circle the subject in the first sentence. Then complete the second sentence with the correct subject pronoun.**

1. (Mrs. Petty) is a teacher. _____*She*_____ teaches English.

2. My father's car is green. _____ is new.

3. John and I are brothers. _____ are both students.

4. Steve and Chuck are cousins. _____ live in Taiwan.

5. My brother Jorge loves sports. _____ plays basketball, soccer, and golf.

6. Ellen and Mark are siblings. _____ share an apartment.

7. My grandmother's house is very old. _____ needs a new roof.

8. My sister and I wear the same size. _____ often borrow each other's shoes.

9. Lenny's aunt and uncle are coming to visit. _____ will stay in a hotel.

10. This bed is small. But _____ is very comfortable.

B **Read the pairs of sentences. Work with a partner. Find the five incorrect sentences and correct them. Cross out the nouns that are replaced by pronouns in those sentences. Remember to capitalize the first word in the sentence.**

1. Pam and Joe just got engaged. Pam and Joe they are already planning their wedding.

2. David is my stepbrother. He David just passed his driving test.

3. Christine and I like to go to the movies. We usually go to a movie on Saturday nights.

4. Andrea is a new student. She is making new friends.

5. Barney and Don are my cousins. They live in Mexico City and share an apartment.

6. Keiko likes to ride her bike to work. She Keiko thinks it is good exercise.

7. My aunt and uncle want to travel. They are planning a trip to Japan.

8. My friend works at a restaurant. He doesn't like his job.

9. Guillaume is my very tall brother. He Guillaume plays basketball.

10. My neighbor is Olivia. She Olivia loves her garden and waters it every evening.

Object Pronouns

Object pronouns (such as *me, him, them*) replace nouns that are the object of a verb. Object pronouns usually come after the verb in a sentence. They replace nouns that have already been mentioned. Do not repeat the noun.

Study the chart. Note that object pronouns can be singular or plural.

Singular Object Pronouns	Examples	Plural Object Pronouns	Examples
me	Alice loves **me**.	us	Nora drove **us** to the airport.
you	Janet helped **you**.	you	She sent **you** a package.
him, her, it	Min called (Mrs. Klein) OBJECT Min called **her**. (her = Mrs. Klein)	them	David emailed (Stan and Joey) OBJECT David emailed **them**. (them = Stan and Joey)

Object pronouns can also come after prepositions, such as *with, at, on, in, for,* and *from.*

Examples:

Lenny sang **with me.**

I mailed a package **to him.**

PRACTICE **A** **Read the pairs of sentences. Complete the second sentence in each pair with the correct object pronoun.**

1. I emailed Mr. Smith. I invited _____ to dinner.

2. I always drive my daughter to the train station. Then, I buy _____ a train

   ticket.

3. Pam thinks about her boyfriend all the time. She misses _____ very much.

4. I bought a new car. I drove _____ to school today.

5. I wanted to make plans with Noriko and Paul. So, I called _____ last night.

6. Teresa always sends me something for my birthday. This year, she sent a beautiful scarf and

   emailed _____.

7. I drive Dave to work every day. I drive _____ because he doesn't have a car.

8. Leo sent Patricia an email. He sent the email to _____ this morning.

9. I would like to play tennis tomorrow afternoon. Can you play with _____

   at 2 P.M.?

10. Denise and Frank are planning a birthday party for their son. They are going to bake a cake

    for _____.

B **Complete the paragraph. Circle the correct subject or object pronoun.**

A Special Photograph Album

I love to look at my grandparents' photograph album. (It / Them) is my favorite thing
                                                 1.

in their house. I really like the pictures of my mother when (she / her) was a little girl.
                                                 2.

(She / Her) looks so cute with her curly hair and big smile. I also like looking at all of
      3.

the different cars my grandfather bought over the years. He loved (they / them), and
                                                   4.

he took very good care of each one. My favorite pictures are the ones of my parents'

wedding. (They / It) are all black and white photos. My mother and father look nervous,
      5.

but (I / me) am sure (we / they) were very happy. The last part of the album is filled
      6.   **7.**

with pictures of (my / me) and my baby brother. I think I look like my mother when
      8.

(she / her) was my age. I am so glad my grandparents made this album.
      9.

GRAMMAR FOR WRITING: Possessive Adjectives

Possessive adjectives (such as *my*, *their*, *his*) show that something belongs to someone or something. Possessive adjectives always come before a noun to show ownership.

Study the chart of possessive adjectives.

Singular Possessive Adjectives	Examples	Plural Possessive Adjectives	Examples
my	**My** sisters are twins.	our	We sold **our** old furniture.
your	**Your** friend is nice.	your	This is **your** dictionary.
his, her, its	Drew is selling **his** car. Donna smiled at **her** mother.	their	The Ortegas painted **their** apartment.

PRACTICE **A** **Complete each sentence with the correct possessive adjective for the underlined words in bold letters.**

1. <u>I</u> like to spend time with _____ brothers.

2. <u>**My sister**</u> is feeding _____ new puppy.

3. <u>My parents</u> love _____ children.

4. <u>Daniel</u> likes to play games on _____ laptop.

5. <u>Yoko and Hiroshi</u> enjoy going out with _____ cousins.

6. <u>My sister</u> works out of _____ house.

7. <u>My cousin Evelyn</u> likes to play with _____ brother.

8. <u>David and I</u> love _____ children.

9. <u>Alicia and her sister</u> enjoy spending time with _____ neighbors.

B **Complete the paragraph with the correct possessive adjectives for the words in bold.**

Welcome, Baby Anna

I live with _____ **Uncle Steve** and _____ family in
            1.   **2.**

Boulder, Colorado. My uncle is a librarian. He works at the Norlin Library at the University

of Colorado. **My uncle** got married two years ago. _____ wife is very nice.
                                                           3.

_____ name is **Micaela**. She is a photographer. Now she is a mother, too.
       4.

Last week, my aunt and uncle had a **baby girl**. _____ name is Anna. I'm
                                                5.

very happy to be an aunt.

WRITING ABOUT YOUR OWN FAMILY

Prewriting

A **Show your family tree to a partner and use it to describe your family.**

B **Answer these questions about your family.**

1. How many people are there in your family? _____

2. What are your parents' names? _____

    Where do they live? _____

3. What does your father do? _____

    What does your mother do? _____

4. How many brothers and sisters do you have? _____

   What are their names? _____

   How old are they? _____

5. Do you have any children? _____ How many? _____

   What are their names? _____

   How old are they? _____

✎ Writing

Ⓐ **Write at least five sentences about your family.**

1. _____

2. _____

3. _____

4. _____

5. _____

Ⓑ **Use your sentences to write a paragraph about your family. Begin by choosing an adjective to complete the first sentence. Remember to follow the rules of paragraph writing. Use at least three pronouns in your paragraph. Also, use at least two possessive adjectives. Give your paragraph a title.**

_____

I have a (big / small / happy) _____

_____

_____

_____

_____

_____

_____

Revising

A Exchange paragraphs with a partner. Read the paragraph your partner wrote. Then use the Revising Checklist to help your partner improve the paragraph.

REVISING CHECKLIST	YES	NO
1. Is the first word of the paragraph indented?		
2. Does each sentence begin with a capital letter and end with a period (or question mark or exclamation point)?		
3. Does each new sentence begin next to the one before it?		
4. Are there at least three pronouns?		
5. Are there at least two possessive adjectives?		
6. Does the paragraph have a title?		

B Use your partner's suggestions to revise your own paragraph. Write your revised paragraph on a separate piece of paper. Put it in your portfolio.

WRITING ABOUT A RELATIVE

Prewriting

A Think about someone in your family you would like to write about.

Write your relative's name here: _____

B Answer these questions about your relative. You can write short answers. You do not need to write complete sentences.

1. How is this person related to you (cousin, sister, brother, etc.)? _____

2. How old is he or she? _____

3. Is he or she married or single? _____

4. Where does he or she live? _____

5. What does he or she do? _____

6. What is one thing he or she likes to do? _____

7. What is one more thing he or she likes to do? _____

C Write one or two more interesting things about your relative.

_____

_____

Writing

A Write four complete sentences about your relative.

1. _____

2. _____

3. _____

4. _____

B Use your sentences to write a paragraph about your relative. Use at least three pronouns and two possessive adjectives in your paragraph. Give your paragraph a title.

_____

My _____ 's name is _____

_____

_____

_____

Revising

A Exchange paragraphs with a partner. Read the paragraph your partner wrote. Then use the Revising Checklist to help your partner improve the paragraph.

REVISING CHECKLIST	YES	NO
1. Is the first word of the paragraph indented?		
2. Does each sentence begin with a capital letter and end with a period (question mark or exclamation mark)?		
3. Does each new sentence begin next to the one before it?		
4. Are there at least three pronouns?		
5. Are there at least two possessive adjectives?		
6. Does the paragraph have a title?		

B Use your partner's suggestions and your own ideas to revise your paragraph on a separate piece of paper. Put it in your portfolio.

GRAMMAR FOR WRITING: Compound Sentences with *And, But*

Sometimes, when you write in English you can combine two simple sentences to make one *compound sentence*. The new sentence will have two subjects and two verbs, and the capital letter in the second sentence changes to a small letter. You can use words such as *and* and *but* to combine the two simple sentences. These words are called *conjunctions*. Put a comma (,) before the conjunction.

Study the chart. Notice the use of *and* and *but*.

Conjunction	Use	Example
and	joins two sentences with similar ideas together	Tom Brower has a close family, **and** he loves them very much.
but	joins two sentences with differing or contrasting ideas	Sandra enjoys spending time with her family, **but** she doesn't get to see them very often.

PRACTICE **A** Read the model paragraph and circle the conjunctions *and* and *but*.

My Best Friend

My best friend's name is José. He is very responsible, and he is also fun to be with. We have a great time whenever we get together. He is smart, and he reads a lot. That's why he always has interesting things to say. He is quite a talkative guy, but he is a very good listener, too. I can talk about my problems with him, and he always gives me good advice. I am really glad to have a friend like José.

B Complete each sentence with *and* or *but*.

1. My brother likes playing tennis, _____ he enjoys swimming.

2. I want to visit my aunt, _____ I don't have enough time.

3. My mother gave me the grocery list, _____ I lost it. I need to call her to see what she wants me to buy.

4. Jason asked his parents for help, _____ he asked his friends, too.

5. Debra doesn't like to cook, _____ her husband, Dave, does. He usually makes dinner.

6. My sister is getting married next month, _____ she is very busy with wedding plans.

7. I want to buy a new camera, _____ I don't have enough money. I need to save more money before I buy one.

8. My cousin takes violin lessons, _____ she plays in the school orchestra.

9. My father works on Saturdays, _____ he doesn't work on Sundays.

10. I am very tired. I want to go to sleep, _____ I have a lot more homework to do. I need a cup of coffee!

C Combine the pairs of sentences using *and* or *but*.

1. Sandra goes out with her cousins. She goes out with her friends, too.

   _____

2. Maria would like to spend more time with her sisters. She is usually too busy.

   _____

3. Erin wants to email her mother. Her computer is broken.

   _____

4. Min sent in her application. She is waiting for the result.

   _____

5. My aunt is from Turkey. My uncle is from Turkey, too.

   _____

D Compare your sentences with a partner's. Did you use the same words to combine the sentences?

WRITING ABOUT A FRIEND

Prewriting

A In small groups, discuss the qualities of a good friend. Put a check (✓) next to the qualities that you think are important. You may add any other qualities you think are important.

_____ responsible	_____ good listener	_____ loyal
_____ fun to be with	_____ honest	_____ friendly
_____ kind	_____ good-looking	_____ helpful
_____ intelligent	_____ wealthy	_____ generous

B Choose a friend to write about. Describe your friend to the people in your group. What qualities does your friend have?

Write your friend's name here: _____

C Answer the questions about your friend. You can write short answers. You do not need to write complete sentences.

1. How old is your friend? _____

2. Is your friend married or single? _____

3. Where does he or she live? _____

4. What does your friend do? _____

5. What does he or she like to do? _____

6. What qualities does your friend have? _____

D Write one or two more interesting facts about your friend.

_____

_____

Writing

A Write six complete sentences about your friend.

1. _____

2. _____

3. _____

4. _____

5. _____

6. _____

B Use some of your sentences to write a paragraph about your friend. Remember to follow the rules of paragraph writing. Use at least three pronouns, two possessive adjectives, and two compound sentences in your paragraph. Give your paragraph a title.

_____

My friend's name is _____

_____

_____

_____

_____

_____

Revising

A Exchange paragraphs with a partner. Read the paragraph your partner wrote. Then use the Revising Checklist to help your partner improve the paragraph.

REVISING CHECKLIST		
	YES	NO
1. Is the first word of the paragraph indented?		
2. Does each sentence begin with a capital letter and end with correct punctuation?		
3. Does each new sentence begin next to the one before it?		
4. Are there at least three pronouns?		
5. Are there at least two compound sentences?		
6. Are there at least two possessive adjectives?		
7. Does the paragraph have a title?		

B Use your partner's suggestions to revise your paragraph. Write your revised paragraph on a separate piece of paper. Put it in your portfolio.

ON YOUR OWN

Write a paragraph on one of these topics. Then use the Revising Checklist to improve your paragraph.

- Write a paragraph about another friend. Use the questions on page 29 to help you get started.
- Talk to one of your younger relatives. Write a paragraph about him or her.
- Talk to one of your older relatives. Write a paragraph about him or her.
- Write about someone you met recently. Where did you meet him or her?
- Think about someone you miss. Write a paragraph about that person.

USE YOUR IMAGINATION

A Pretend it is the year 2030. Make a list of sentences about your family in 2030. Think about their children, careers, and homes.

Examples:

I have a son named Stephen. He is a math teacher.

My daughter's name is Diana. She is the mayor of my hometown.

1. _____

2. _____

3. _____

4. _____

5. _____

B Choose an adjective such as *wonderful, small, large,* or *unusual* to describe your family in 2030, and complete the first sentence. Then use your sentences from Exercise A to write a paragraph. Add a title.

_____

I have a(n) _____ *family.* _____

_____

_____

_____

_____

_____

YOU BE THE EDITOR

The paragraph below has five mistakes with pronouns. With a partner, find and correct the mistakes.

My Cousin

My cousin's name is Bettina Lee. She is thirty-seven years old. She was born in Chicago, Illinois, but now her lives in Denver, Colorado. She is married and has two children. Bettina and me enjoy spending time together. Us love to go ice-skating. Bettina is an excellent ice-skater. She skated in ice shows when he was young. Now, Bettina teaches ice-skating to young children. She enjoys watching their.

REAL-LIFE WRITING: Writing an Email

Writing email messages is a quick and easy way to communicate with family and friends. Emails are usually short and specific.

A   **Read the sample email.**

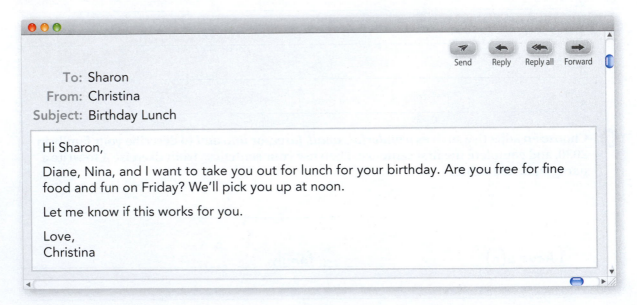

To: Sharon
From: Christina
Subject: Birthday Lunch

Hi Sharon,

Diane, Nina, and I want to take you out for lunch for your birthday. Are you free for fine food and fun on Friday? We'll pick you up at noon.

Let me know if this works for you.

Love,
Christina

B   **Write an email for each of the following situations.**

1. Write an email to your roommate, Juanita. Remind her to stop at the pizza shop on her way home and get a large mushroom pizza.

To:
From:
Subject:

2. Write an email to your friend, Paul. Tell him that you are sorry, but you will not be able to meet him for dinner tonight. Ask him if tomorrow night is good for him.

To:
From:
Subject:

3. Write an email to your coworker, Jong. Tell him your car broke down. Ask him to give you a ride to work tomorrow morning.

LEARNING OUTCOMES

Paragraph Writing: Write a paragraph about your free-time activities

Real-Life Writing: Write an email inviting a friend to do something with you

WRITING ABOUT ACTIVITIES YOU LIKE TO DO

A Look at the five pictures. They show activities a student named Eric likes to do with his friends. Write the name of the activity under the correct picture. Use words from the word bank.

ACTIVITIES WORD BANK		
go out to dinner	go to the movies	play video games
go to concerts	play soccer	

1. _____

2. _____

3. _____

4. _____

5. _____

B Read the model paragraph about what Eric likes to do in his free time.

Spending Time with Friends

In his free time, Eric likes to do things with his friends. He often plays soccer with his friends after class. On the weekends, he likes to go out to dinner or go see a movie with them. Eric and his friends go to concerts, too. Sometimes they don't go anywhere, but they aren't bored. They play video games, or they just sit around and talk and laugh. Eric always has fun when he is with his friends.

C Talk to a partner. Ask and answer these questions.

1. What does Eric like to do in his free time?

2. What do Eric and his friends like to play after class?

3. What else does Eric like to do with his friends?

GRAMMAR FOR WRITING: The Simple Present Tense

We use the *simple present tense* to write about daily activities, repeated actions, and things that are usually true.

Examples:

*Our class **begins** every day at 9 A.M.*

*Yumi often **takes** the bus to class.*

Study the chart. Notice the forms of the simple present tense verbs.

Subject	Simple Present Tense Verb	Rest of Sentence
I	write	short stories.
Zumi	plays	volleyball with her friends.
They	visit	their grandparents on the weekends.

PRACTICE **A** Draw a circle around the subject of each sentence. Underline the simple present tense verb.

1. I ride my bike for exercise.

2. She plants many kinds of flowers in her garden.

3. It snows a lot here in January.

4. He exercises at the gym.

5. They watch TV in the evenings.

6. We play tennis every weekend.

7. Cho and Lisa eat lunch in the cafeteria.

8. He collects stamps from all over the world.

9. You play the piano very well.

10. Chris listens to music on his cell phone.

B Look at the sentences again. The *base form* of the verb is the infinitive form without *to*. It is sometimes called the *simple form*. Which subjects use the base form of the verb? Write them.

_____

C Which subjects use the *-s* form of the verb?

_____

D Work with a partner. Complete the two rules.

1. Use the *-s* form of the verb when the subject of the sentence is

_____

2. Use the *base form* of the verb when the subject of the sentence is

_____

Third Person Singular of the Simple Present Tense

Study the spelling rules for verbs in the simple present tense.

Verb Ending	Examples
For most verbs: add **-s to the base form**	work → work**s** play → play**s**
When the base form of the verb ends in a consonant + *y*: change the **y** to **i** and add **-es**	wor**ry** → wor**ries**
When the base form of the verb ends in *s, z, ch, sh,* and *x*: add **-es**	toss → toss**es** tou**ch** → tou**ches**
Some verbs are irregular. You need to learn the forms of these verbs.	be → **am / is / are** do → **do / does** have → **have / has**

Read the sentences with the verb _be_. Circle the verb and then answer the questions.

a. I am a member of the chess club.

b. You are a good tennis player.

c. He is the captain of the soccer team.

d. Sam is a good cook.

e. She is a hockey coach.

f. The window is open.

g. It is an old house.

h. We are on the volleyball team.

i. You are busy on the weekends.

j. They are good photographers.

k. Jane and Chris are great dancers.

1. Which subject uses _am_?_____

2. Which subjects use _is_?_____

3. Which subjects use _are_?_____

B **Read the sentences with the verb _have_. Circle the verb in each sentence. Then complete the two rules.**

a. I have several hobbies.

b. You have fun after school.

c. He has a good time on the weekends.

d. Isabelle has plans with Jose.

e. She has lots of friends.

f. The book has rules to many card games.

g. The gym has a new pool.

h. We have tickets to the movie.

i. You have enough money to travel.

j. They have time to go to a movie.

k. Tadashi and Alexis have a good time with their friends.

1. Use _has_ when the subject of the sentence is _____

_____

2. Use _have_ when the subject of the sentence is _____

_____

C Read the sentences with the verb *do*. Circle the verb in each sentence. Then complete the two rules.

a. I do lots of activities with my friends.

b. My daughter does the dishes after dinner.

c. He does twenty sit-ups every day.

d. Isabelle does well in many sports.

e. She does the laundry on Saturday.

f. It does a good job taking videos.

g. We do the shopping.

h. You do a lot of research on the Internet.

i. I do my homework right after class.

j. Herman James and Frank Brandon do the work together.

1. Use *do* when the subject of the sentence is _____

_____

2. Use *does* when the subject of the sentence is _____

_____

Forming Negatives in the Simple Present Tense

Study the chart. Notice the forms of the negative simple present tense.

Rule	Examples
Use **does not** or **doesn't** before the base form of regular verbs with *he, she, it* and singular subjects.	He **doesn't** work. Billy **doesn't** enjoy card games.
Use **do not** or **don't** before the base form of the verb with *I, we, you, they* and plural subjects.	They **do not (don't)** work on the weekends. I **do not (don't)** want to watch that TV show. You **do not (don't)** sleep late on weekdays. We **do not (don't)** have time to go to the movie. Kathy and Sharon **do not (don't)** work on the weekends. They **do not (don't)** get up early.
Add the word **not** after the correct form of the verb **be.** The short (contracted) forms are: **'m not, isn't, aren't.**	I **am not** busy today. (**I'm not** busy today.) You **are not** late. (You **aren't** late.) He **is not** a good tennis player. (He **isn't** a good tennis player.) It **is not** time to go. (It **isn't** time to go.) We **are not** bored. (We **aren't** bored.) They **are not** soccer fans. (They **aren't** soccer fans.)

Underline the simple present verbs in the paragraph.

Playing Team Sports

I play several team sports. During the summer, my friends and I are on a soccer team. We play every Wednesday afternoon and Saturday morning. I am the captain of the team. My older brother is the coach. Our families watch the games. They always cheer when we score a goal. During the fall, I play lacrosse for my school team. I'm not very good, but I have a lot of fun. We play teams from other schools. My parents usually come to the games. They enjoy watching me play. During the winter, I play on a club basketball team. I practice shooting baskets every day after school. Our team is very good. We often win the championship. As you can see, team sports are one of my favorite activities.

B **Read the paragraph "Playing Team Sports" again. Look at the subject + simple present tense verbs in the paragraph. Write the subjects + verbs below.**

1. I play
2. _____
3. _____
4. _____
5. _____
6. _____
7. _____
8. _____
9. _____

10. _____
11. _____
12. _____
13. _____
14. _____
15. _____
16. _____
17. _____
18. _____

C **The sentences below have mistakes with simple present verb forms. Correct the sentences.**

1. Maria don't stay home on Saturday nights.

   Maria doesn't stay home on Saturday nights.

2. We plays soccer on the weekend.

   _____

3. You isn't ever on time.

_____

4. She wash her clothes every week.

_____

5. My sisters likes action movies.

_____

6. I has lots of new friends in my class.

_____

7. I no think he watches too much TV.

_____

8. She aren't on the swim team.

_____

9. He don't like loud music.

_____

10. They doesn't eat out during the week.

_____

D **Rewrite the paragraph. Change _I_ to _Sally_. Change the verbs and pronouns as necessary.**

Free Time Activities

I like to spend my free time outdoors. I don't like to stay inside when the sun is shining. My favorite outdoor activity is gardening, and I love to plant new kinds of flowers in my garden every year. I don't have time during the week, but I like to go to the park on weekends. I enjoy taking long walks in the park and riding my bike there. On sunny days, I go to the beach with my friends. As you can see, I love being outside in my free time.

Sally likes to spend her free time outdoors. _____

_____

_____

_____

_____

Forming *Yes / No* Questions in the Simple Present Tense: Regular Verbs

Yes / no questions in the simple present are formed with **do** or **does** and the **base form of the main verb**. Begin the *yes / no* question with **do** or **does**, and then add the **subject** and **main verb**. Remember to end the question with a question mark (?).

Examples:

Do I have *time to watch this movie?*

Do you dance *well?*

Does he play *the piano?*

Does she work *hard?*

Does it break *easily?*

Do we have *fun together?*

Do they belong *to the same team?*

PRACTICE **Change the sentences to *yes / no* questions. Write the question on the line.**

1. Maria plays games with her children.

   _____

2. Dan plays soccer on the weekend.

   _____

3. You work on the weekends.

   _____

4. She washes her clothes every week.

   _____

5. Their brothers enjoy jazz.

   _____

6. We use social media every day.

   _____

7. She has a lot of friends.

   _____

8. He likes to go to the movies.

   _____

Forming *Wh-* Questions in the Simple Present Tense: Regular Verbs

Wh- questions are questions about *who*, *what*, *when*, *where*, *why,* and *how*. Begin a *wh-* question with a question word. Then add *do / does* + *subject* + *base form of the main verb*. Remember to end with a question mark (?).

Examples:

Who do you text?

Where does he study English?

When do they play video games?

What does she do in the summer?

 PRACTICE   **A**   Work with a partner. Write four *wh-* questions in the simple present tense about your partner's activities on the weekends. You can also ask questions about the activities of people your partner knows.

1. _____

2. _____

3. _____

4. _____

B   Exchange papers and write answers to your partner's questions.

1. _____

2. _____

3. _____

4. _____

PARTS OF A PARAGRAPH

In Chapter 1, you learned that a paragraph is a group of sentences that communicates one main idea. Most paragraphs have three parts: a *topic sentence*, several *supporting sentences*, and a *concluding sentence*.

- The *topic sentence* is the most important sentence in the paragraph. It is often the first sentence in the paragraph. The topic sentence tells the reader what the paragraph is about.

- Next come the *supporting sentences*. These sentences give details, examples, and reasons to explain the topic sentence. All of the supporting sentences must relate to the topic of the paragraph.

- Some paragraphs end with a *concluding sentence.* The concluding sentence restates the main idea in different words. Here are some common ways to begin a concluding sentence:

  All in all,   *As you can see,*   *In conclusion,*

It may be helpful to think of a paragraph as a sandwich. The topic and concluding sentences are like the top and bottom pieces of bread. The supporting sentences are like the lettuce, tomatoes, cheese, and meat that you put between the pieces of bread.

Topic Sentence

Supporting Sentences

Concluding Sentence

PRACTICE **Work with a partner. Read each paragraph and think about the parts. Then answer the questions.**

1.

Playing Games

    I love to play games. I enjoy games that you play with other people, such as card games and board games. I especially like games that make you think hard. That's why my favorite game is chess. I also like games that you can play alone, such as solitaire and sudoku. Naturally, I like playing games on my computer or smartphone, too. All in all, I think games are fun and challenging.

   a. What is the topic sentence? Circle it.

   b. How many supporting sentences are there? _____

   c. What is the concluding sentence? Underline it.

2.

My Hobbies

    I have several hobbies that keep me busy in my free time. I love to read, and I often read short stories and magazines. Another one of my hobbies is cooking, and Chinese cooking is my specialty. My favorite hobby is photography. I usually take black-and-white pictures because I think they are more interesting than color pictures. In conclusion, my life would not be as much fun without my hobbies.

   a. What is the topic sentence? Circle it.

   b. How many supporting sentences are there? _____

   c. What is the concluding sentence? Underline it.

3.

> ## Free Time in the City
>
> I live in a big city, so there are many things to do in my free time. One thing I really enjoy is trying different kinds of restaurants. I also like going to concerts and listening to new bands. Even if I don't have any extra money, I love to go shopping. Sometimes, I just like to sit at a café and watch people. With so many choices, I often have a hard time deciding what to do in my free time.

a. What is the topic sentence? Circle it.

b. How many supporting sentences are there? _____

c. What is the concluding sentence? Underline it.

WRITING ABOUT YOUR FREE TIME

 Prewriting

A Talk to a partner. What do you like to do in your free time? What do you like to do with your friends or family? What do you like to do alone?

FREE-TIME ACTIVITIES WORD BANK		
bake	go to concerts	play computer games
collect stamps	go to museums	play sports
cook	go to parties	read
dance	go to the beach	sew/knit
do arts and crafts	listen to music	sing
draw	paint	swim/ski/surf
exercise/work out	play an instrument	talk on the phone
garden	play board games (chess, backgammon)	take pictures
go shopping		take walks

B Make a list of the activities you like to do in your free time.

_____   _____

_____   _____

_____   _____

C Share your list with your partner. Talk about the activities you like the most. Do you and your partner like to do any of the same things? Which ones?

 **Writing**

A Use your list to complete each of the sentences.

1. I like to _____

2. I also like to _____

3. Another thing I enjoy is _____

4. I don't enjoy _____

5. I like to _____, and I _____

6. I enjoy _____, but I _____

7. I don't like to _____, but I _____

B Use your sentences to write a paragraph. Complete the topic sentence. Then write three or four supporting sentences, and complete the concluding sentence. Add a title.

_____

In my free time, I _____

_____

_____

_____

_____

_____

_____

_____

_____

As you can see, _____

_____

Revising

A Exchange paragraphs with a partner. Read the paragraph your partner wrote. Then use the Revising Checklist to help your partner improve the paragraph.

REVISING CHECKLIST	YES	NO
1. Does each sentence begin with a capital letter and end with correct punctuation?		
2. Does each new sentence begin next to the one before it?		
3. Is there a topic sentence?		
4. Are there three or four supporting sentences?		
5. Does the concluding sentence restate the main idea?		
6. Is the simple present tense used correctly?		

B Use your partner's suggestions to revise your paragraph. Write your revised paragraph on a separate piece of paper. Put it in your portfolio.

WRITING ABOUT YOUR GROUP

 Prewriting

Work in a small group. Ask the people in your group questions about their free-time activities. Complete the chart with each person's favorite free-time activities.

Name	Favorite Free-Time Activities

Writing

A Write five sentences based on the information in the chart.

1. _____

2. _____

3. _____

4. _____

5. _____

B Use your sentences to complete the paragraph. Include four or five supporting sentences. Complete the concluding sentence.

The people in my group like to do many things in their free time.

_____

_____

_____

_____

_____

_____

_____

As you can see, _____

🔍 Revising

A Use the Revising Checklist to help you improve your paragraph.

REVISING CHECKLIST		
	YES	NO
1. Does each sentence begin with a capital letter and end with correct punctuation?		
2. Does each new sentence begin next to the one before it?		
3. Is there a topic sentence?		
4. Are there three or four supporting sentences?		
5. Does the concluding sentence restate the main idea?		
6. Is the simple present tense used correctly?		

B Exchange paragraphs with a partner. Read the paragraph your partner wrote. Then use the Revising Checklist to help your partner improve the paragraph.

WRITING ABOUT STAYING HEALTHY

A Look at the pictures. They show activities that people do and habits people have to stay healthy. Discuss the pictures with a partner. Use the words and phrases from the word bank.

HEALTHY HABITS AND ACTIVITIES WORD BANK

do yoga	get checkups	ride a bike
eat nutritious foods	get eight hours of sleep	work out

1  **2**  **3**

4  **5**  **6**

B Complete the sentences. Use vocabulary from the word bank in Exercise A. Use the correct form of the verb in simple present tense.

1. Ari _____, such as fruits and vegetables, to stay healthy.

2. Farah _____ two miles to school every day.

3. Liz _____ at her doctor's office at least once a year.

4. Martin always _____ a night.

5. Sophia _____ at the gym four times a week.

6. Cassie _____ every evening to relax.

C Read the paragraph. Underline the topic sentence and the concluding sentence. Circle the simple present verbs.

Staying Healthy

I do several things to stay healthy. First of all, I exercise regularly. I work out at the gym four times a week. I also ride my bike to school and play tennis on the weekends. In addition, I am careful about my diet. For example, I eat lots of fruits and vegetables, and I avoid junk food. I also try to get eight hours of sleep every night. Most importantly, I quit smoking! All in all, staying healthy is important to me.

WRITING ABOUT YOUR HEALTHY ACTIVITIES AND HABITS

 Prewriting

A Work with a group of three or four students. Discuss the questions.

1. Do you exercise regularly? How often do you exercise?

2. What kind of exercises do you do?

3. Do you eat healthy meals? What kinds of food do you think are good for you? What kinds of food do you think are not very good for you?

4. Do you smoke? If so, how much and when do you smoke?

5. Do you usually get enough sleep at night? How many hours of sleep do you usually get? How much sleep do you need?

B Write five ways you try to stay healthy. Add your ideas to the list.

Ways I Stay Healthy

1. *I do not smoke cigarettes.*

2. _____

3. _____

4. _____

5. _____

6. _____

C Compare your list with another student's. Do you have any of the same ideas? Which ones are the same?

Writing

A Choose one of these topic sentences.

- I do several things to try to stay healthy.
- There are several ways to stay healthy.

B Write a paragraph. Use some of the ideas from your list for at least three supporting sentences. End your paragraph with a concluding sentence. Add a title.

_____

_____

_____

_____

_____

_____

_____

 **Revising**

A Exchange paragraphs with a partner. Read the paragraph your partner wrote. Then use the Revising Checklist to help your partner improve the paragraph.

REVISING CHECKLIST		
	YES	NO
1. Does each sentence begin with a capital letter and end with correct punctuation?		
2. Does each new sentence begin next to the one before it?		
3. Is there a topic sentence?		
4. Are there three or four supporting sentences?		
5. Does the concluding sentence restate the main idea?		
6. Is the simple present tense used correctly?		

B Use your partner's suggestions to revise your paragraph. Write your revised paragraph on a separate piece of paper. Put it in your portfolio.

ON YOUR OWN

Write a paragraph on one of these topics. Use the simple present tense. Then use the Revising Checklist to improve your paragraph.

- Talk to several people in your family about what they like to do in their free time. Write a paragraph about one person's free time.
- Talk to several people in your family or your friends about what they do to stay healthy. Write a paragraph about how one of the people stays healthy.
- Find someone who has an unusual hobby or interest. Write about what that person likes to do in his or her free time.

YOU BE THE EDITOR

The paragraph below has seven mistakes with simple present tense verbs. With a partner, find and correct the mistakes.

A Tired New Mother

I am a proud, but tired mother of twin baby boys. I don't has any free time these days. My days am very busy, and my nights are busy, too. I never gets much sleep anymore. I wake up several times during the night to feed the babies. They is always hungry! So, I am tired in the morning. I try to take naps when the babies are napping, but I have so much to do. I wash baby clothes and blankets every morning and evening. I also changes diapers all day long. Sometimes when both babies cries at the same time, I cry, too. But when I watches them sleeping peacefully, I know how lucky I am to have two happy, healthy babies.

REAL-LIFE WRITING: Writing an Email

A   **Read the sample email.**

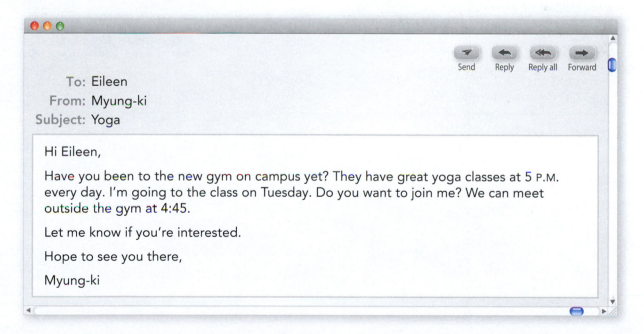

To: Eileen
From: Myung-ki
Subject: Yoga

Send   Reply   Reply all   Forward

Hi Eileen,

Have you been to the new gym on campus yet? They have great yoga classes at 5 P.M. every day. I'm going to the class on Tuesday. Do you want to join me? We can meet outside the gym at 4:45.

Let me know if you're interested.

Hope to see you there,

Myung-ki

B Write an email to your friend. Choose an activity that you like to do, such as playing a sport, having dinner at a favorite restaurant, riding bikes in the park, going to the beach, or going to a club or party. Invite your friend to join you.

C Exchange your email with a partner. Write a response to your partner's email.

....
LEARNING OUTCOMES
....

Paragraph Writing: Write a paragraph about how to make or do something

Real-Life Writing: Write a recipe card for a favorite recipe

WRITING ABOUT HOW TO MAKE OR DO SOMETHING

A Look at the pictures. They show the steps to make a yogurt milkshake. Read the steps. Match each step to the correct picture. Write the letter.

1. __b__

2. _____

3. _____

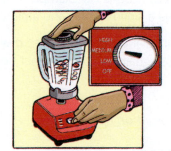

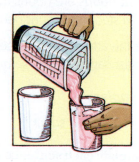

4. _____

5. _____

6. _____

a. Then cut up some fresh fruit such as bananas, peaches, mangoes, or strawberries.

b. First, take out 1 cup of yogurt, 2 cups of milk, and 2 tablespoons of honey.

c. Add the fruit to the yogurt, milk, and honey in the blender.

d. Pour the yogurt, milk, and honey into a blender.

e. Finally, pour the milkshake into glasses and enjoy your nutritious snack.

f. Put the top on the blender and blend on medium for two minutes.

B Use the steps in Exercise A to complete a paragraph about how to make a yogurt milkshake.

How to Make a Yogurt Milkshake

When you want a delicious and healthy snack, try this yogurt milkshake.

_____

_____

_____

_____

After you see how easy it is to make a yogurt milkshake and taste how

delicious it is, you'll want to share the recipe with your friends.

GRAMMAR FOR WRITING: Count Nouns and Noncount Nouns

A *noun* is a word that names a *person*, *place*, *thing*, *activity*, or *idea*. Nouns may be the subject of a sentence, the object of a verb, or the object of a preposition.

There are two kinds of nouns in English: *count nouns* and *noncount nouns*. Most nouns are count nouns. Many learners's dictionaries will tell you if a certain noun is a count noun (countable) or a noncount noun (uncountable).

Count Nouns

Count nouns are nouns that you can count. For example, one *cup*, two *pencils*, five *chairs*, twenty-seven *students*. Count nouns have a singular form and a plural form.

Use the articles *a* or *an* before singular count nouns. Use *a* with singular count nouns that begin with a consonant sound. Use *an* with singular count nouns that begin with a vowel sound.

Examples:

*Do you have **a** snack?*   *I want **an** apple.*

PRACTICE Complete each sentence with *a* or *an*.

1. Can I borrow _____ egg?

2. He needs _____ peach for the milkshake.

3. Cut up _____ apricot.

4. Did you make _____ snack?

5. He added _____ olive to the salad.

6. I'm saving my money to buy _____ new blender.

7. Have you ever made _____ apple pie?

8. I want to learn how to make _____ milkshake.

Forming the Plural of Count Nouns

Most count nouns form the plural by adding -s or -es, but some count nouns require spelling changes.

Study the chart. Notice how to form the plural of count nouns.

Type of Noun	How to Form the Plural	Examples
Most nouns	Add **-s**.	banana ➙ banana**s** cup ➙ cup**s** snack ➙ snack**s**
Nouns that end in *ch, s, sh, ss,* and *x*	Add **-es**.	lun**ch** ➙ lunch**es** wi**sh** ➙ wish**es** cla**ss** ➙ class**es** bo**x** ➙ box**es**
Nouns that end in a consonant + *y*	Change the **y** to **i** and add **-es**.	berr**y** ➙ berr**ies** cit**y** ➙ cit**ies** famil**y** ➙ famil**ies**
Nouns that end in *o*	Add **-es**.	mang**o** ➙ mang**oes** potat**o** ➙ potat**oes** tomat**o** ➙ tomat**oes**
Nouns that end in *f*	Change *f* to **v** and add **-es**.	hal**f** ➙ hal**ves** wol**f** ➙ wol**ves** loa**f** ➙ loa**ves**
Nouns that end in *fe*	Change *f* to **v** and add **-s**.	kni**fe** ➙ kni**ves** li**fe** ➙ li**ves** wi**fe** ➙ wi**ves**

In addition, there are some count nouns that have an irregular plural form.

child ➙ children	man ➙ men	person ➙ people	tooth ➙ teeth
foot ➙ feet	mouse ➙ mice	radio ➙ radios	woman ➙ women

Remember: Use the singular form of the verb with singular count nouns as subjects. Use the plural form of the verb with plural count nouns as subjects.

Examples:

This child **needs** *help.*   *This banana* **tastes** *sweet.*

These children **need** *help, too.*   *These bananas* **taste** *sweet, too.*

PRACTICE **A** Underline the plural nouns in the paragraph "How to Make a Yogurt Milkshake" on page 56.

B Complete the sentences. Use the plural form of a word from the list.

glass	loaf	strawberry
knife	potato	tooth

***Example:** I used two glasses of milk.*

1. She added some _____ to her milkshake.

2. You need to peel all the _____ before you boil them.

3. I baked three _____ of bread.

4. These _____ are very sharp. Be careful!

5. I brush my _____ after every meal.

Noncount Nouns

Noncount nouns are things that we can't or don't usually count. Noncount nouns have only one form. They do not have singular or plural forms. Sentences that have noncount nouns as a subject always use the third person singular form of the verb.

We do not use *a* or *an* with noncount nouns. Instead, we use phrases with noncount nouns that tell us quantity, such as *a lot of, a little, some*.

• Use *some* with noncount and plural count nouns to indicate an uncertain or unspecified amount.

• Use *a lot* for noncount and plural count nouns to indicate many, or a large number. Note that *a lot* is followed by *of* when the noun is mentioned.

• Use *a little* for noncount nouns to indicate a small number.

Study the chart with categories and examples of common noncount nouns. Work with a partner to add two additional examples of noncount nouns for each category. Then share your words with the class.

Categories	Examples
food	bread, butter, cheese, chicken _____ _____
liquids	coffee, juice, milk, soup _____ _____
school subjects	chemistry, English, history, math _____ _____
abstract ideas	anger, beauty, knowledge, love _____ _____

Categories	Examples
natural events	lightening, heat, humidity, sunshine _____ _____
materials	glass, cloth, wool, plastic _____ _____
others	furniture, homework, information, advice _____ _____

PRACTICE **A** **Read the sentences. Correct the mistakes. One sentence is correct. Circle it.**

1. I am studying a cooking.

2. I need some advices about how to make hamburgers.

3. I did my homeworks last night.

4. He added some salt to the soup.

5. Do you have informations about this recipe?

6. The baby drinks a lot of milks every day.

Examples:

I put **some sugar** in my coffee.   We have **a lot of homework**.

He likes **a little milk** in his tea.   We have **a lot**.

B Write *a, an,* or *some* before each noun.

1. I just got _____ email from Richard with the recipe for making chocolate

    brownies.

2. My friend gave me _____ advice about baking bread.

3. I want to add _____ peach to this milkshake.

4. Cook this chicken in _____ oil.

5. She has _____ information about the recipe for you.

6. This soup needs _____ salt. Be careful. Don't add too much.

7. I have _____ fruit to add to the salad.

8. Add the juice of _____ orange.

9. I'll send you _____ text with the instructions.

C Complete each sentence with *a little* or *a lot*.

1. This cookbook has _____ of good recipes.

2. I need to borrow _____ butter for the cake I'm making.

3. This coffee needs _____ sugar.

4. We have _____ of fruit. Please take some.

5. I want to make orange juice for my whole family. I need to buy _____ of oranges.

6. I can help you bake the cookies this afternoon. I have _____ time between classes.

7. You need _____ of eggs to make this quiche.

8. Put _____ oil in the pan and heat it for two minutes.

Noncount Nouns with Measurement Words

Sometimes you may want to describe specific quantities of noncount nouns in your writing. Then you need to use a measure word. Some common measure words include: *bottle, bowl, box, can, container, cup, gallon, glass, jar, liter, loaf, piece, pound, slice, tank, tablespoon, teaspoon.*

Study the chart with measurement words and examples of common noncount nouns that go with them. Work with a partner. Add two additional examples of noncount nouns for each category. Then share your words with the class.

Measurement Word	Noncount Nouns	
cup of teaspoon of tablespoon of	sugar flour _____	_____
glass of	milk water _____	_____
piece of	fruit cake _____	_____
bowl of	cereal rice _____	_____

Complete each sentence with the correct measurement word from the chart.

1. It's so hot. I'd love a _____ of juice.

2. Can I have a _____ hot chocolate?

3. I take one _____ of honey in my tea.

4. I usually have a _____ of oatmeal for breakfast.

5. Would you like a _____ of cherry pie for dessert?

6. If you have the hiccups, you should drink a _____ of water.

TIME-ORDER PARAGRAPHS

You have already learned several important things about paragraphs. You know that a paragraph has a special form. You also know that a paragraph has three parts: a topic sentence, supporting sentences, and a concluding sentence. It is also important to learn how to organize the supporting sentences in an English paragraph. There are several common ways to do this. One way to organize the supporting sentences is to use *time order*. That means organizing your ideas in the order in which they happen.

PARAGRAPH POINTER: Signal Words

Many paragraphs include **signal words** to connect ideas in a paragraph. Signal words help guide the reader from one idea to the next. When you want to explain how to do something, the first thing you need to do is make a list of the steps in the process. Then you arrange the steps according to time order. When you write your paragraph, use time-order signal words to make the order of the steps clear to the reader. Here is a list of some time-order signal words:

first/first of all	*next*	*finally*
second/secondly	*then*	
third	*after that*	

 A **Look at the cartoon. Read the caption (the words under the picture) and underline the time-order signal words.**

"Licking your paws is only the first step.
After that, you need to use a good antibacterial
body wash, then an exfoliating herbal facial scrub,
followed by an avocado moisturizing cleanser."

B Complete the paragraphs using time-order signal words.

1.

How to Photograph a Cat

It's not hard to get a good picture of your cat if you follow these steps. _____, give your cat something to eat. When she is full, move your cat to a sunny window. _____, rub your cat's back for a few minutes until she falls asleep. Do not make any loud noises. As soon as she wakes up, get in position and have your camera ready. _____, take the picture as she yawns and stretches.

2.

How to Get a Driver's License

In order to get a driver's license in the United States you need to follow these steps. _____, go to the Department of Motor Vehicles in the state where you live and fill out an application. _____, study for and take an online or paper test on the traffic signs and driving laws. _____ you have to take and pass a vision test. _____, you need to take a road test. The person who gives you the test will make sure that you can drive safely. Once you pass the road test, you will get your driver's license.

3.

How to Use *Live Search Maps*

It's easy to get driving directions from one place to another on the Internet using a site called *Live Search Maps*. _____, open *Live Search Maps* and click the icon that says "Directions." _____, type into the "Start" box the address or location where you will begin your trip. _____, type into the "End" box the address of your destination. At this point, you can choose your route. To choose the quickest way, click "Shortest Time." To choose the shortest way, click "Shortest Distance." _____, click "Get Directions" and you will get step-by-step directions from your starting point to your destination. Hopefully, you won't get lost.

GRAMMAR FOR WRITING: Imperative Sentences

An *imperative sentence* is a special kind of sentence that expresses an instruction, a command, or a request. When we give someone instructions, we often use imperative sentences.

You have learned that a complete sentence must have a **subject** and a **verb**. In an imperative sentence the subject is always *you*, but it is not stated. It is understood. Imperative sentences begin with the base form of a verb and end with a period (.). Sometimes an imperative sentence can end with an exclamation point (!).

For negative imperative forms, use: **Do + not** (or **Don't**) + **base form** of the main verb.

Study the chart. Notice the verbs in imperative sentences.

Affirmative Imperatives	**Press** the start button **Close** the door. **Add** the sugar.	**Complete** the form. **Slow down!**
Negative Imperatives	**Don't** add salt.	**Do not** add salt.

PRACTICE **A** Circle the imperative verbs in the paragraph "How to Make a Yogurt Milkshake" on page 56.

B Underline the imperative verbs in the paragraphs that follow.

1.

How to Avoid Jet Lag

Here are several steps you can follow to avoid jet lag. First of all, get a good night's sleep the night before you travel. Secondly, set your watch to the time of your destination when you get on the plane. Then, drink plenty of water during the flight. Don't drink alcohol or caffeine. Also, move around during the flight. Walk around the plane or do some simple stretching exercises in your seat. When you arrive at your destination, keep busy. Do not take a nap. Finally, eat meals and go to bed when the local people do.

2.

How to Make Perfect Hard-boiled Eggs

You can make perfect hard-boiled eggs if you follow these steps. First, take the eggs out of the refrigerator and let them come to room temperature. Then, put the eggs in a pan with enough water to cover them by at least an inch. Bring the water to a boil. Turn off the heat as soon as the water boils and cover the eggs for about 15 minutes. Next, put the eggs in a bowl with cold water and a few ice cubes. Let the eggs cool for 10 minutes. Finally, you are ready to peel the eggs and enjoy eating them.

WRITING PARAGRAPHS THAT GIVE INSTRUCTIONS

A Look at the pictures. They show the steps to remove an ink stain. Work with a partner. Read the list of steps, and number the steps in the correct time order.

1.

2.

3.

4.

5.

_____ Second, spray the stain with hair spray.

_____ Finally, wash the piece of clothing as usual.

_____ Third, rub the stain gently with a clean cloth.

_____ Continue rubbing until the stain is completely gone.

_____ First, put a paper towel under the stain.

B Read the topic sentence. Then use the steps in Exercise A to complete the paragraph.

How to Remove an Ink Stain

This is what you need to do to remove an ink stain from clothing.

_____

_____

_____

_____

_____

_____

_____

C Look at the pictures. They show the steps to stop a nosebleed. Work with a partner. Read the list of steps, and number the steps in the correct time order.

1.

2.

3.

4.

5.

_____ Second, use a cotton pad or tissue to catch the blood.

_____ Pinch the soft part of your nose with your thumb and index finger for ten minutes.

_____ If your nose continues to bleed, call a doctor.

_____ Then, sit down with your head leaning forward.

_____ First, loosen the clothing around your neck.

D Read the topic sentence. Then use the steps in Exercise C to complete the paragraph.

How to Stop a Nosebleed

You should follow these steps to stop a nosebleed. _____

_____

_____

_____

_____

E Look at the pictures. They show the steps in carving a pumpkin. Work with a partner, read the list of steps, and number the steps in the correct time order.

1.

2.

3.

4.

5.

6.

7.

_____ Next, draw a pattern for the face on the pumpkin with a felt-tip pen.

_____ Then, gently push out the cut-out features to the inside of the pumpkin.

_____ Finally, place a small candle inside the pumpkin.

_____ First, you need to cut a hole in the top. To do this, draw a circle about six inches in diameter on top of the pumpkin around the stem.

_____ Use a smaller knife to carefully carve out the face you drew on your pumpkin.

_____ Second, use a large, sharp knife to cut around the circle and remove the top.

_____ After that, scoop out the seeds and pulp from inside the pumpkin with a large spoon.

F Read the first two sentences. Then use the steps in Exercise E to complete the paragraph.

How to Carve a Pumpkin

Carving a pumpkin for Halloween is fun, but it is also messy. So, make sure you have covered your work area with newspaper before you begin.

_____

_____

_____

_____

_____

_____

_____

_____

_____

_____

_____

WRITING ABOUT HOW TO MAKE OR DO SOMETHING

 Prewriting

A Choose one of the following topics to write about.
- how to send an email
- how to pack for a weekend trip
- how to make a good salad
- how to fall asleep
- how to mend a broken heart
- how to cure the hiccups
- how to treat a cold
- how to convert from Celsius to Fahrenheit (or other metric to English measurements)

B Make a list of all the steps for the topic you chose. Then number the steps in time order.

_____	_____
_____	_____
_____	_____
_____	_____
_____	_____

Writing

A Write the steps in complete sentences. Use the imperative for some of the sentences.

1. _____

2. _____

3. _____

4. _____

5. _____

B Complete this topic sentence about your process.

It is _____ to _____.
    (easy / fun / hard, etc.)

C On a separate piece of paper, write a paragraph giving instructions. Include a topic sentence, imperative sentences, time-order signal words and a title.

Revising

A Exchange paragraphs with a partner. Read the paragraph your partner wrote. Then use the Revising Checklist to help your partner improve the paragraph.

REVISING CHECKLIST	YES	NO
1. Is there a topic sentence?		
2. Are the sentences in correct time order?		
3. Are there signal words to help guide the reader?		
4. Are the imperative sentences used correctly?		
5. Are the plural nouns formed correctly?		
6. Are the count and noncount nouns used correctly?		

B Share your paragraph with your classmates. Put your paragraph in your portfolio.

ON YOUR OWN

Write a paragraph on one of these topics. Give your paragraph a title and put it in your portfolio.

- how to clean something (your room, your car, etc.)
- how to fix something (a flat tire, a broken vase, etc.)
- how to cook or bake something
- how to play something (checkers, soccer, etc.)
- one of the other paragraph topics from the list on page 67

YOU BE THE EDITOR

The paragraph below has six mistakes with singular and plural nouns and count and noncount nouns. With a partner, find and correct the mistakes.

A Delicious Drink

Turkish coffee is not easy to make, but it is delicious. There are several way to make Turkish coffee, but this is the way my friend taught me. First, you need a special pot called a *cezve*. Pour 3 cup of cold water into the pot. Then, add 3 teaspoons of coffee and 3 teaspoons of sugars to the water. Next, heat the waters on a low flame until you can see foam forming on top. Don't let it boil. Then, take the pot off the heat. Gently stir the mixture and return it to the heat. Repeat this two more time. Finally, pour the coffees into 3 cups. Make sure each person gets some foam and enjoy your coffee.

REAL-LIFE WRITING: Writing a Recipe Card

A   Fill out a recipe card for one of your favorite dishes. First, make a list of the ingredients. Then write the instructions for how to prepare the dish. Use words from the word bank to help you.

COOKING WORD BANK

bake	chop	cut	grill	mix	sauté
boil	combine	fry	heat	peel	simmer
broil	cook	garnish	melt	pour	stir

Recipe for: _____

Ingredients: _____   _____

_____   _____

_____   _____

_____   _____

Instructions: _____

_____

_____

_____

_____

_____

_____

_____

B Prepare the dish and bring it to class to share with your classmates. Put your recipe card in your portfolio.

C After you have tried your classmates' dishes, pick your favorite one. Ask your classmate for the recipe. If your classmate agrees, copy the recipe for that dish onto the recipe card below. Add the card to your portfolio.

Recipe for: _____

Ingredients: _____   _____

_____   _____

_____   _____

_____   _____

Instructions: _____

_____

_____

_____

_____

_____

_____

_____

Paragraph Writing: Write a paragraph about a special or typical day

Real-Life Writing: Write a message on a greeting card

WRITING ABOUT A TYPICAL DAY

Ⓐ **Look at the pictures. They show a typical day in the life of a man named Roberto Trevino. Find the sentence that matches each picture. Write the letter of the sentence under the correct picture.**

1. _b_

2. _d_

3. _g_

4. _f_

5. _e_

6. _h_

7. _g_

8. _c_

3 **a.** Roberto teaches from 8:30 A.M. to 3:30 P.M.

1 **b.** He wakes up at 7:00 A.M. to eat breakfast and get dressed.

8 **c.** Finally, Roberto goes to bed at midnight.

2 **d.** Then he takes the 7:45 A.M. train to the school where he teaches computer science.

5 **e.** At 6:00 P.M., he eats dinner with his wife.

4 **f.** He takes the train back home at 4:00 P.M.

7 **g.** He plays the saxophone from 8:00 P.M. to 10:00 P.M. Sometimes he sings, too.

6 **h.** At 7:30 P.M., he arrives at The Jazz Club.

B **Use the sentences in Exercise A to complete a paragraph about a typical day in Roberto's life. The topic sentence and concluding sentences are given.**

Roberto's Busy Days

Roberto's days are very busy.

- He wakes up at 7:00am to eat breakfast and get dressed.
- Then he takes the 7:45am train to the school where he teaches computer science.
- Roberto teaches From 8:30am to 3:30pm
4 He takes the train back home at 4:00pm
5. At 6:00pm, he eats dinner with his wife.
6. At 7:30pm, he arrives at The Jazz Club
7. He plays the saxophone From 8:00pm to 10:00pm Sometimes he sings, too.
8. Finally, Roberto goes to bed at midnight.

As you can see, Roberto has a very busy life.

GRAMMAR FOR WRITING: Prepositions of Time

Prepositions are small but important words in English. It is important to use the correct preposition when you write.

Prepositions come before nouns in a sentence. One important use is to express time. We use many different prepositions to talk about time. The most common are **on**, **in**, and **at**.

Study the chart of prepositions used with time words.

Preposition	Time Words	Examples
on	+ day of the week + day of the week + part of a day + a specific date	I go to work **on** Monday. I take an English class **on** Tuesday evening. She was born **on** April 30.
in	+ a month + a season + a part of the day Exception: *at night*	She was born **in** April. We have fun **in** the summer. I do my homework **in** the afternoon. I do my homework **at** night.
at	+ a specific time	My English class starts **at** 9:30.
from . . . to	+ a specific time or date to a specific time or date	Mr. Morimoto exercises **from** 5:30 **to** 6:30 every morning.
for	+ a period of time	He exercises **for** an hour.

PRACTICE **A** **Look at the cartoon. Circle the prepositions and time words. Underline the simple present tense verbs. Talk with a partner. Do you think the cartoon is funny? Why or why not?**

Copyright Randy Glasbergen
www.glasbergen.com

"On Mondays, I get ready to plan my week. On Tuesdays,
I plan my week. On Wednesdays, I revise my plan for the week.
On Thursdays, I put my plan for the week into my computer.
On Fridays, I think about starting my plan for next week."

B **Complete the sentences with the correct preposition of time.**

1. I take an English class __on__ Wednesday afternoon.

2. She has to work late __on__ Monday.

3. Mohammed goes to work __at__ 9:00.

4. Cheng goes to school __in__ the morning.

5. I sent the email __on__ January 29.

6. I study __for__ three hours every day.

7. I like to watch TV __at__ night.

8. I have classes __from__ 10:00 __to__ 4:30.

9. The new semester starts __in__ January.

10. He wakes up __from__ 7:30 __to__ the morning.

C **Complete the paragraph with the correct prepositions of time.**

My Busy Day

My days are very busy. I wake up __at__ 6:30 A.M. and take my dog for a walk.
                                   1.

Then, I eat breakfast, get ready for school, and make my lunch. I usually ride my bike to

school. I have classes __from__ 9 A.M. __to__ 3 P.M. Then, I study at the library __in__ the
                        2.   **3.**   **4.**

afternoon. I also have a part-time job. I wash dishes at a restaurant near campus. I work

__from__ 6 P.M. __to__ 9 P.M. The job is not bad. I like the people I work with. I also get a
5.   **6.**

free dinner! __at__ 9 P.M., I ride my bike home. I take my dog for another walk. Then, I
            7.

relax. I often watch TV __for__ an hour. Sometimes, I read or listen to music. Finally, I get
                        8.

ready for bed.

GRAMMAR FOR WRITING: Frequency Adverbs

Frequency adverbs are used to tell how often something happens. The most common frequency adverbs are *always*, *usually*, *often*, *sometimes*, *rarely*, *seldom*, and *never*. Use the simple present tense when you use frequency adverbs to write about your daily activities and habits.

• Frequency adverbs usually come after the verb *be*.

Examples:

*I am **rarely** in a bad mood.*   *He **is always** tired.*   *They **are usually** late for parties.*

• Frequency adverbs usually come before all other verbs.

Examples:

*She **often** goes to bed late.*   *We **seldom** eat out.*   *We **always** listen to the news.*

Raramente

Study the chart. Notice the position of frequency adverbs in sentences.

Frequency Adverbs	Examples
always (100% of the time)	I don't have a car. I **always** take the bus to work. I am **always** on time for work.
usually	He **usually** gets up at 7 A.M. He is **usually** on time for class.
often	We **often** go for a walk after dinner. We are **often** tired after our walk.
sometimes (50% of the time)	I **sometimes** drink coffee after dinner. I am **sometimes** late for work. Note: *Sometimes* can also come at the beginning of a sentence. **Sometimes** I am late for work.
rarely	Meryl is on a diet. She **rarely** eats dessert. We are **rarely** home during the day.
seldom	Hakeem **seldom** goes to bed before midnight. He is **seldom** tired before midnight.
never (0% of the time)	Feride is a vegetarian. She **never** eats meat. I am **never** late for class.

PRACTICE **A** **Read the paragraph. Underline the frequency adverbs.**

A Busy Doctor

Dr. Gary Lesneski is an obstetrician. An obstetrician is a doctor who delivers babies. Dr. Lesneski <u>usually</u> gets up at six thirty in the morning. He goes to his office at seven o'clock. His workdays are <u>never</u> typical, but they are <u>always</u> busy. He <u>never</u> knows what time a baby will be born. <u>Sometimes</u> babies are born in the afternoon. <u>Sometimes</u> they are born at night. He <u>often</u> has to go to the hospital in the middle of the night. He <u>rarely</u> sleeps through an entire night without any interruptions. Dr. Lesneski loves his work, but he looks forward to his vacation in August.

B **Work in groups of three. Find out how often your classmates do each activity. Complete the chart. Use the words in the word bank to help you.**

FREQUENCY ADVERBS WORD BANK

always	never	often	rarely	seldom	sometimes	usually

	You	Name	Name
	Liza.		
get up early	usually		
eat lunch at a restaurant	rarely	rarely	
take a bus to school or work	never		
study in the library	often		
take a nap in the afternoon	sometimes		
watch TV in the evening	always		
be late for school or work	never		
use social media	always		
go to bed late	seldom		
read a printed newspaper	never		
read the news online	never		
check email and text messages	always		

C Write sentences based on information in the chart in Exercise C.

Examples:

I usually get up early.

Nari rarely eats lunch at a restaurant.

1. I never take a bus to school or work.
2. I often study in the library
3. Sometimes I take a nap in the afternoon
4. I always watch tv in the evening.
5. I never be late for school or work.
6. I always use media social
7. I seldom go to bed late
8. I never read a printed newspaper
9. I never read the news online
10. I always check email and text messages

GRAMMAR FOR WRITING: *Before* and *After*

You can combine sentences with ***before*** and ***after*** to show time order. Notice the comma (,) in the middle of the sentence when a sentence starts with ***Before*** or ***After***.

Study the chart. Notice how the following sentences are combined with *before* and *after*.

First, I brush my teeth. Then, I go to bed.

Time Word	Examples
before	**Before** I go to bed, I brush my teeth. I brush my teeth **before** I go to bed
after	**After** I brush my teeth, I go to bed. I go to bed **after** I brush my teeth.

Combine the pairs of sentences using *before*. Use a comma when necessary.

1. First, I wash my hands. Then, I eat dinner.

   I wash my hands before I eat dinner.

2. First, I do my homework. Then, I watch TV.

   Before I watch TV, I do my homework

3. First, I go to the gym. Then, I do my homework.

   I go to the gym **before** I do my homework.

4. First, I eat breakfast. Then, I read the newspaper.

   Before I read the newspaper, I eat breakfast.

5. First, I do the dishes. Then, I relax.

   I do the dishes before I relax

6. First, I check my email. Then, I look at my text messages.

   Before I look at my text messages, I check my email

B Combine the pairs of sentences using *after*. Use a comma when necessary.

1. First, I get home from work. Then, I take my dog for a walk.

   After I get home from work, I take my dog for a walk.

2. First, I eat dinner. Then, I wash the dishes.

   After I eat dinner, I wash the dishes.

3. First, I get to school. Then, I have coffee with my friends.

   I have coffe with my friends **after** I get to school.

4. First, I read my son a story. Then, I put him to bed.

   After I read my son a story, I put him to bed

5. First, I turn on my laptop. Then, I check my email.

   I check my email after I turn on my laptop.

6. First, I revise my paragraph. Then, I put it in my portfolio.

   After I revise my paraprah, I put in my portofolo

C Complete the sentences about yourself.

1. After I get dressed in the morning, I _go to the college_

2. After I get to school (work), I _Come back For my son._

3. Before I do my homework, I _play whrt my husband and son_

4. Before I make dinner, I _do my homework._

5. Before I turn off my computer, I _check my e-mail._

6. _I always pray_ before I go to sleep.

7. _I make lunch_ after I leave school.

8. _I speak with my mother_ before I eat dinner.

9. _I read a book_ after I write a paragraph.

TIME-ORDER PARAGRAPHS

When you write a paragraph about your day or week, you should also use *time order* to organize the sentences. Begin with what you do first. Then write about what you do second, and so on. You can use signal words to make the order clear to your reader. Review the time-order signal words you learned in Chapter 4, along with some new ones.

TIME-ORDER SIGNAL WORD BANK			
after	first	second	after breakfast
after that	first of all	then	after school
before	later	third	before work
finally	next		in the morning/afternoon/evening

A Read each group of sentences. Write *TS* for topic sentence. Then number the supporting sentences so they are in correct time order. Finally, write the sentences in paragraph form. Add your own concluding sentence.

1. _____ Every morning at 6:00 A.M. he goes to the flower market to buy flowers.

   _TS_ Mr. Park owns a busy flower shop.

   _____ After the store closes, Mr. Park always delivers flowers.

   _____ He usually works there from 9:00 A.M. to 4:00 P.M.

   _____ Then he drives to his shop.

Mr. Park's Day

_____

_____

_____

_____

2. _____ Then I go to classes for about five hours.

_____ My typical day is pretty busy.

_____ After my classes, I go to work at the university library.

_____ I always wake up early so I can read the newspaper, eat breakfast, and check my email and text messages.

_____ At 7:00 P.M., I usually meet my friends for dinner.

My Busy Day

_____

_____

_____

_____

3. _____ She always goes to the gym in the morning.

_____ Next, she goes to work at a clothing store from 5:00 P.M. to 9:00 P.M.

_____ Then she takes classes at the university in the afternoon.

_____ Maria is very active during the summer.

_____ After the store closes, Maria often goes out with her coworkers.

Maria's Active Summer

_____

_____

_____

_____

B   **Read the model paragraph.**

Lazy Sundays

I am usually very lazy on Sundays. I get up late, and I eat a big breakfast. After breakfast, I read the newspaper for a few hours. Sometimes I talk to my friends on the telephone. At four o'clock, I am usually hungry, so I make a snack. Then I watch TV or take a nap. In the evening, I often go out to dinner with my friends, but I am back in bed again at ten o'clock. I like to relax on Sunday so that I am ready to start my week on Monday.

1. Draw a circle around the topic sentence of the paragraph.

2. Underline the supporting sentences.

3. Draw a circle around the concluding sentence of the paragraph.

C   **Rewrite the paragraph in Exercise B. Change *I* to *Jason*. Make all the other necessary changes in pronouns and verbs.**

Lazy Sundays

Jason is _____

_____

_____

_____

_____

_____

_____

_____

PARAGRAPH POINTER: Paragraph Unity

You have learned that a paragraph is about one main idea. All of the supporting sentences in a paragraph must be about the main idea in the topic sentence. A sentence that does not support the main idea does not belong in the paragraph. When all of the sentences support the main idea, the paragraph has *unity*.

A **Cross out the sentence that does not support the main idea. Then read the explanation.**

Boring Days

During the week, my days are boring. I get up at 7:00 A.M. every day. Then I get dressed for school. Even that is boring because I have to wear a uniform to school. I always have the same thing for breakfast, fruit and yogurt, because it's fast and healthy. I take the bus to school where I spend the next seven hours. My schedule of classes is the same every day. ~~My Spanish teacher is from Mexico.~~ After school, I take the bus home and practice my violin for an hour. Finally, I do my homework and study. Luckily, my weekends are much more exciting.

Notice: The topic sentence, *During the week, my days are boring*, states the main idea of the paragraph. All of the other sentences should explain that idea. The sentence *My Spanish teacher is from Mexico* is true, but it is not about the student's boring days. It should not be included in this paragraph.

B **One sentence in each paragraph does not belong. First underline the topic sentence. Then read the paragraph and cross out the sentence that does not belong.** → Pertenecer.

1.

Water Activities

I love the water. I learned how to swim when I was just five years old. ~~I have two younger sisters.~~ Swimming is one of my favorite activities to do in the water. I also like sailing on lakes and scuba diving in the ocean. Besides having fun in the water, I am interested in the plants and animals that live in water. That's why I am studying marine biology. As you can see, I love the water, and I hope one day I can work in or around it.

2.

An Athletic Person

Ben is a very athletic person. He loves to play all types of sports. Ben's favorite sport is volleyball. He belongs to a volleyball club where he can play with other people. Ben also likes to run and swim for exercise. He belongs to a gym where he exercises at least four times a week. ~~Ben also works at the library.~~ Ben certainly keeps himself busy with all of the athletic activities he does during the week.

WRITING ABOUT YOUR TYPICAL WEEKDAY

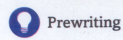 Prewriting

A Draw simple pictures that show what you do on a typical weekday. Fill in the clock with the time you wake up.

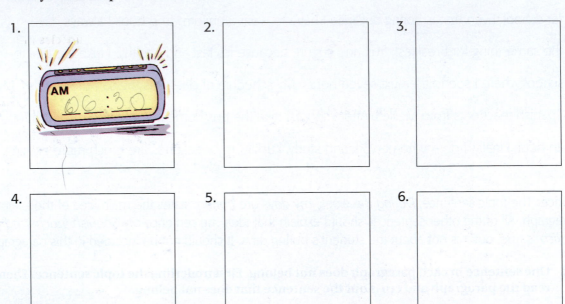

1.

2.

3.

4.

5.

6.

B Write questions to ask a partner about a typical weekday. Talk to your partner and ask and answer each other's questions. Write the answers. Use your drawings to describe your typical day.

1. _____

_____

2. _____

_____

3. _____

_____

4. _____

_____

5. _____

_____

6. _____

_____

Writing

A Write a sentence to go with each picture you drew in Prewriting Exercise A. Use a frequency adverb in at least three sentences. Use words from the word bank to help you.

WEEKDAY ACTIVITIES WORD BANK		
brush my teeth	get up/wake up	read articles online
check my email	go to bed	read the newspaper
do homework	listen to music	shave
do the dishes	make (eat/have) breakfast (lunch/dinner)	take a shower/bath
drive to school/work	make the bed	use social media
get dressed	put on makeup	watch TV
get ready for bed		

1. _____

2. _____

3. _____

4. _____

5. _____

6. _____

B Write a paragraph about a typical day. Use your sentences from Writing Exercise A. Use at least three frequency adverbs in your paragraph. Add a concluding sentence. Write a title for your paragraph.

_____

During the week, my days are very (busy/boring/interesting).

_____

_____

_____

_____

_____

_____

 **Revising**

A Exchange paragraphs with a partner. Read the paragraph your partner wrote. Then use the Revising Checklist to help your partner improve the paragraph.

REVISING CHECKLIST	YES	NO
1. Is the title written correctly?		
2. Does each sentence begin with a capital letter and end with correct punctuation?		
3. Does the paragraph have a topic sentence and a concluding sentence?		
4. Are the sentences in correct time order?		
5. Are all of the sentences about the main idea?		
6. Are there at least three frequency adverbs?		
7. Are prepositions of time used correctly?		

B Use your partner's suggestions to revise your paragraph. Write your revised paragraph on a separate piece of paper. Put it in your portfolio.

WRITING ABOUT SPECIAL DAYS

Not all days are typical. Some days are special. Think about special days in your life and holidays in your culture.

A Discuss these questions in small groups.

1. How do you celebrate birthdays in your culture?

2. What are the most important holidays in your country?

B Discuss this question. Complete the chart.

What is your favorite day of the year? Why?

NAME	FAVORITE DAY

C Read the paragraph a student wrote about her favorite holiday.

My Favorite Holiday

My favorite holiday is Songkran, the traditional Thai New Year. We celebrate Songkran in the spring, from April 13 to April 15. Businesses, schools, and banks are usually closed. Many people who live in big cities go back to their hometowns for three days to celebrate with their family and friends. At the beginning of Songkran, we clean our houses. Next, we cook traditional Thai food such as pad Thai for our family and friends. We often wear new clothes, and then we go to the temple to pray and give food to the monks. Young people sprinkle water on their parents' and grandparents' hands to show respect. After that, the real fun begins. Everyone goes outdoors. There are always parades and beauty contests in the streets. Children and adults stand on the side of the road and throw water on people passing by. In fact, Songkran is famous for splashing water and even water fights. It is very hot, so people rarely mind getting wet. All over Thailand, Songkran is a time for fun, family, and getting wet. If you plan to visit Thailand during Songkran, make your hotel reservations early. Also, leave your camera in your hotel room because it will get wet!

D Underline the verbs in the simple present tense in the paragraph "My Favorite Holiday."

E Circle the time-order signal words and frequency adverbs in "My Favorite Holiday."

WRITING ABOUT A HOLIDAY

 Prewriting

Ask and answer these questions with a partner.

1. What is your favorite holiday?

2. When do you celebrate it?

3. Are businesses open or closed?

4. How do you celebrate this holiday?

5. Who do you celebrate it with?

6. What special foods do you eat?

7. What do you wear?

8. Where do you go to celebrate?

9. Do you give or receive gifts?

10. Why do you like this holiday?

 Writing

A **Write answers to the questions about your favorite holiday in the Prewriting activity. Use complete sentences. Use frequency adverbs and time prepositions in at least three sentences.**

1. _____

2. _____

3. _____

4. _____

5. _____

6. _____

7. _____

8. _____

9. _____

10. _____

B Write a paragraph about your favorite holiday. Use your sentences from Writing Exercise A as a guide. Add any other information that will make your paragraph more interesting. Use frequency adverbs and time-order signal words. Remember to begin with a topic sentence and include a title.

_____

_____

_____

_____

_____

_____

_____

_____

_____

_____

_____

Revising

A Exchange paragraphs with a partner. Read the paragraph your partner wrote. Then use the Revising Checklist to help your partner improve the paragraph.

REVISING CHECKLIST		
	YES	NO
1. Is the first word of the paragraph indented?		
2. Does each sentence begin with a capital letter and end with correct punctuation?		
3. Does the paragraph have a topic sentence?		
4. Is the title written correctly?		
5. Are all of the sentences about the main idea?		
6. Are the frequency adverbs used correctly?		
7. Does the paragraph include time-order signal words?		
8. Are the prepositions of time used correctly?		

B Use your partner's suggestions to revise your paragraph. Write your revised paragraph on a separate piece of paper. Put it in your portfolio.

YOU BE THE EDITOR

The paragraph below has five mistakes with prepositions of time. With a partner, find and correct the mistakes.

A Busy Pharmacist and Mother

I am a pharmacist and a mother, and my days are busy. As a pharmacist, my job is to prepare and sell medicines. Every morning, I get up on 6:30 A.M. I have breakfast with my family and make lunch for my daughter to take to school. I leave the house at 8:00 A.M. and drive to the drugstore where I work for 9:00 A.M. at 5:00 P.M. During the day, I fill prescriptions for customers. Sometimes the customers have questions about their medicines. I answer their questions. I also give them information about how often to take the medicine. After work, I drive home and have dinner with my family. Then I help my daughter with her homework during a few hours. Sometimes I read or watch TV at the evening before I go to bed. I am very busy, but I really enjoy being a pharmacist and a mother.

ON YOUR OWN

Write a paragraph on one of these topics. Then use the Revising Checklist on page 89 to improve your paragraph. Give your paragraph a title and put it in your portfolio.

- Write a paragraph about a typical day of one of your classmates.
- Write a paragraph about a typical day of someone in your family.
- Write a paragraph about a recent birthday you have celebrated.
- Write a paragraph about your favorite holiday when you were a child.

REAL-LIFE WRITING: Writing a Message on a Card

A   Do you like to send cards to your friends and family? Look at the front of this card. Read the message inside. Who is this card for? Why did she receive this card?

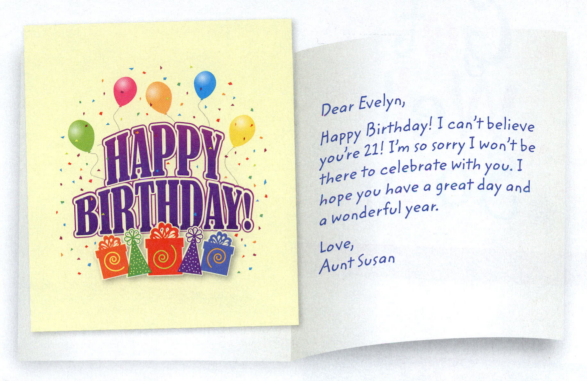

Dear Evelyn,

Happy Birthday! I can't believe you're 21! I'm so sorry I won't be there to celebrate with you. I hope you have a great day and a wonderful year.

Love,
Aunt Susan

B   Read the front of these cards. Write a two- or three-sentence message on the inside to someone you know.

Paragraph Writing: Write a descriptive paragraph about a person or thing
Real-Life Writing: Complete an order form; write a lost and found message

DESCRIBING PEOPLE

A Look at the pictures of people waiting for a train. Match each person to a description on page 94. Write the correct letter under each person.

1. _a._   2. _d_   3. _b_   4. _c_   5. _e_

Ileva

a. Mr. Wilcox is a tall, thin, middle-aged man. He is bald and has a black mustache. He wears big glasses. Today, he is wearing a blue jacket and a striped tie. He is carrying a briefcase. He is reading a train schedule.

b. Sally is a slender young woman of average height. She has long, straight, blond hair and a beautiful smile. Today, she is wearing a black and red plaid coat and black leather boots. She is carrying her laptop in a shoulder bag. She is talking on a cell phone.

c. Dennis is a short young man with a round face and curly red hair. He has big green eyes, freckles, and a dimple in his chin. Today he is wearing his favorite yellow T-shirt and sweatpants. He is carrying a dark green backpack.

d. Tom is a good-looking teenager. He is average height and weight. He has straight, black hair and brown eyes. Today, he is wearing a green sweatshirt and corduroy pants. He is also wearing a red baseball cap and a new pair of white sneakers. He is listening to music on his phone.

e. Elif is an attractive woman. She has long, wavy, brown hair and big beautiful eyes. Today, she is wearing a grey jacket, black pants, and a pink turtleneck. She's also wearing a silver necklace and long earrings.

B **Study the two word banks. Then look at the two pictures. Write a short description of each person. Use words from the two word banks.**

PHYSICAL CHARACTERISTICS WORD BANK

Hair	Eyes	Build	Face	Age	Height
bald	blue	average	beard	in his / her 20s, 30s, 60s	average
black	brown	heavy	dimple		short
blond	dark	medium	freckles	elderly	tall
braids	green	petite	heart-shaped	middle-aged	
brown	hazel	plump	mole	old	
curly / straight	narrow	slender	mustache	teenage	
dark	oval	small	oval	young	
long / short	round	stocky	round		
ponytail		strong	square		
red		thin	wrinkles		
shiny					
short					
shoulder-length					
thick / thin					

CLOTHING AND PERSONAL ITEMS WORD BANK				
Clothes	Jewelry	Footwear	Accessories	Outerwear
blazer	bracelet	boots	backpack	coat
dress	earrings	pumps	baseball cap	jacket
jeans	necklace	sandals	belt	raincoat
pajamas	ring	shoes	glasses	
pants		slippers	gloves	
shirt / blouse		sneakers	hat	
shorts		socks	mittens	
skirt			purse / handbag	
sports jacket			scarf	
suit			sunglasses	
sweater			tie	
sweatpants			umbrella	
sweatshirt			wallet	
T-shirt			watch	
turtleneck				
vest				

1. The man is a tall, He
wears glasses. he is wearing
a brow pants and grey
blazer. He has red shoes.

2. The women has black
leather boots. She is
wearing a bracelet and
purple sweater.

GRAMMAR FOR WRITING: Present Progressive

You have learned that the **simple present tense** is used to describe things that are generally true and don't change.

Examples:

Josh **is** tall.   He **has** black hair and brown eyes.   Teresa **wears** contact lenses.

The **present progressive** is used to describe things that are happening now. It often is used to describe what people are doing or wearing now. The present progressive has two parts: the verb **be** (in the simple present), and **the -ing form of the main verb**. The present progressive is often used with expressions of time such as: **now**, **at the moment**, **today**, **this morning**, **this afternoon**, **this evening**.

Examples:

Sam **is waiting** for a bus right now.   He **is wearing** a raincoat today.

Study the charts. Notice the forms of the present progressive verbs.

STATEMENTS			
Subject	Simple Present of *be*	*-ing* form of main verb	Rest of sentence
I	am (not)	wearing	a hat.
You	are (not)	wearing	a coat.
He / She	is (not)	wearing	gloves.
It	is (not)	raining	now.
We	are (not)	wearing	uniforms.
They	are (not)	wearing	shorts.

You can use contractions in informal situations.

Examples:

I**'m wearing** a hat. I**'m not wearing** gloves.

You**'re wearing** a winter coat. You **aren't wearing** a raincoat. or You**'re not wearing** a raincoat.

He**'s** / She**'s** wearing gloves. He / She **isn't wearing** mittens. or He**'s** / She**'s not wearing** mittens.

It**'s raining** now. It **isn't snowing**. or It**'s not snowing**.

We**'re wearing** uniforms. We **aren't wearing** street clothes. or We**'re not wearing** street clothes.

They**'re working** hard. They **aren't taking** a break. or They**'re not taking** a break.

Yes/No Questions in the Present Progressive

To ask a **yes / no question**, begin with a form of **be** (*am, is* or *are*) + the **subject**, followed by the **-ing form of the main verb**, and finally the rest of the question. End the question with a question mark (?).

Simple Present of *be*	Subject	*-ing* form of main verb	Rest of sentence
Am	I	wearing	a hat?
Are	you	buying	new boots?
Is	he / she	knitting	a scarf?
Are	we / they	wearing	uniforms?

Wh- Questions in the Present Progressive

To ask a **wh- question**, start with the **wh- word**, then add the correct form of **be** (*am, is* or *are*) + **the subject**, followed by the **-ing form of the main verb**, and the rest of the question.

Wh- word	Simple Present of *be*	Subject	*-ing* form of main verb	Rest of sentence
What	are	you	wearing	to the party?
What	is	he / she	reading	now?
Where	are	you	riding	your bicycle?
Who	are	they	meeting	today?

Spelling Rules for Adding *-ing* to Verbs

Verb Ending	Examples	
One consonant + *e*: drop the **-e** and add **-ing**	give ➤ giv**ing**	take ➤ tak**ing**
Two consonants: add **-ing**	lend ➤ lend**ing**	fall ➤ fall**ing**
One vowel + one consonant: double the last consonant and add **-ing**	beg**in** ➤ begi**nning**	r**un** ➤ ru**nning**

Verb Ending	Examples	
Exception: verbs ending in *w, x,* or *y*	Exception: show ➤ show**ing**	
Two vowels + one consonant: add **-ing**	sl**eep** ➤ sleep**ing**	w**ear** ➤ wear**ing**

A Read the descriptions of the people in Exercise A on page 94. Underline the present progressive verbs in each description. Circle the simple present verbs.

B Look at the picture below. What is the woman doing? What are the other people doing? What are they wearing? What are the animals doing? Discuss the picture in small groups. Then write four sentences about the picture using the present progressive.

1. <u>The woman is wearing a long-sleeved sweater and a long skirt.</u>

2. She is feeling the pigeon.

3. The children is playing.

4. The man is stealing the bag.

5. The men is riding bicicle.

JUST FOR FUN

A Have a fashion show. Work with a partner. Make a list of the clothes and accessories your partner is wearing. Use the words from the Clothing and Personal Items Word Bank on page 95 to help you. Ask your teacher for help with any other vocabulary.

_____   _____

_____   _____

_____   _____

B Pretend your partner is a model in a fashion show and you are the announcer. Write sentences that describe what your partner is wearing.

1. _____

2. _____

3. _____

4. _____

5. _____

6. _____

C Choose another classmate to describe. Write a paragraph that describes what the person looks like and what he or she is wearing.

_____

_____

_____

_____

_____

_____

_____

_____

GRAMMAR FOR WRITING: Adjectives

An *adjective* is a word that describes a noun or a pronoun. When you write descriptions, you should use adjectives. Adjectives help your reader "see" the person, place, or thing you are describing. Using adjectives will make your writing more interesting.

Read the rules about using adjectives in English.

Rule	Examples
Adjectives have the same form whether they describe singular or plural nouns.	adjective singular noun She is wearing a **new** jacket. adjective plural noun They are wearing **new** jackets.
Adjectives come before nouns.	He has **brown** eyes. They are wearing **old** sneakers.
Adjectives can come after the verb *be*.	His eyes are **brown**. My purse is **old**. I am **young**.

Some adjectives describe what you think about something or somebody. These are called *opinion adjectives*. You can use these adjectives to describe most nouns.

OPINION ADJECTIVES WORD BANK

attractive	brilliant	nice
awful	excellent	strange
bad	good	ugly
beautiful	important	unusual
boring	interesting	wonderful

Other adjectives give *factual* information about a person, place, or thing. These adjectives describe the size, color, age, shape, condition, or origin of something or someone.

Examples:

*She has **long, black** hair.*

The words *long* and *black* are factual adjectives that describe the size and color of the noun *hair*. They answer the question, "What kind of hair?"

*She has **beautiful, long, black** hair.*

When you add *beautiful* to the sentence, you add an opinion about the noun *hair*.
Notice that the opinion adjective (*beautiful*) comes before the factual adjectives (*long, black*).

*He is wearing an **ugly, old, green** sweater.*

The words *ugly*, *old* and *green* are adjectives that describe the noun *sweater*. They answer the question, "What kind of sweater?" Notice that the opinion adjective (*ugly*) comes before the factual adjectives (*old, green*).

 PRACTICE **A**   **Draw a box around the adjectives in the descriptions in Exercise A on page 94.**

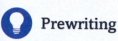 **B** **Read what a student wrote to describe her appearance. Underline the adjectives.**

My name is Jenny Marsh. I am tall and thin. I have long, black hair and big, brown eyes. I usually wear small, round glasses. Today, I am wearing grey, wool pants and a soft, yellow sweater. I am also wearing an old brown belt, and beautiful, new, white sneakers.

DESCRIBING YOURSELF

Prewriting

A **Attach a recent photo of yourself. Think about words you can use to describe yourself.**

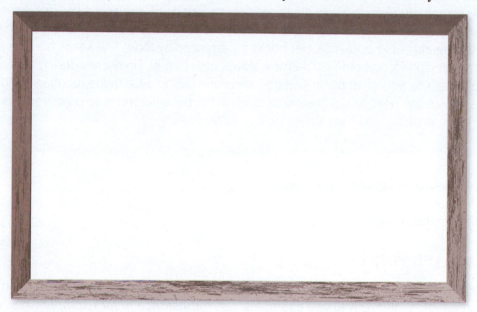

B **Answer these questions about the photo.**

1. What color eyes do you have? _____

2. What color hair do you have? _____

3. What length is your hair? _____

4. Are you tall, short, or average height? _____

5. What are you wearing? _____

6. What kind of shoes are you wearing? _____

7. Are you wearing anything new? _____

8. Are you wearing anything old? _____

 **Writing**

A Use the answers to the Prewriting Exercise B questions to write a description of yourself on a separate piece of paper. Use at least five adjectives. Do not put your name on the paper.

B Fold your description in half and give it to your teacher. Your teacher will give your paper to another student who will try to guess who wrote the description. A well-written description should make it easy for your classmates to identify you.

DESCRIBING A PERSON'S CHARACTER

Read the paragraph that a student wrote about her roommate. Then discuss the questions with a partner.

An Organized Roommate

My roommate Akiko is a very organized person. First of all, she keeps her closet very neat. For example, all of her clothes are arranged by color, and her shoes are neatly arranged on the shelf. She also organizes her bookcase. Her books are arranged by topic. She keeps her CDs in her bookcase in alphabetical order so they are always easy to find. Finally, her desk is very organized. For instance, she puts all of her important papers and bills in a file in the top drawer. The top of her desk is always neat, too. Sometimes I laugh at her because she is so organized. However, she never loses anything, and I am always looking for something.

1. What is the main idea of the paragraph?

2. What examples support the main idea?

PARAGRAPH POINTER: Examples

Remember that all paragraphs need sentences that support the topic sentence. A good way to support a topic sentence is to give *examples*. Use *for instance* or *for example* when you give an example.

PRACTICE **A** Find an example in column B to support each topic sentence in column A. Write the number.

A	B
1. My mother is always busy.	a. _____ She only buys things that are on sale.
2. My roommate is a messy person.	b. _____ He is an amazing painter.
3. My friend is very thrifty.	c. _____ She always has a new joke to tell.
4. Carla is a funny person.	d. _____ She has three part-time jobs.
5. John is a creative person.	e. _____ He leaves his dirty clothes on the floor.

B Write four pairs of sentences based on the sentences in Exercise A. Begin the second sentence of each pair with *For example* or *For instance*.

1. <u>My mother is always busy. For example, she has three part-time jobs.</u>

2. _____

3. _____

4. _____

5. _____

C Complete the sentences with your own ideas. Use examples.

1. My friend is very serious. For example, _____

2. My mother is the kindest person I know. For instance, _____

3. My neighbor gets angry very easily. For example, _____

4. My younger brother is really funny. For instance, _____

5. My teacher is _____. For example, _____

DESCRIBING A PERSON YOU KNOW

 Prewriting

Think of a person you know well. Circle adjectives that describe the person.

PERSONALITY WORD BANK			
ambitious	funny	nervous	selfish
artistic	generous	optimistic	sensitive
boring	hardworking	organized	serious
brave	helpful	patient	shy
competitive	honest	pessimistic	social
creative	jealous	polite	studious
dependable	kind	quiet	talkative
energetic	lazy	responsible	thrifty
enthusiastic	messy	romantic	
friendly	neat	rude	

Make a Cluster Diagram

A cluster is a group of things that are similar. Making a *cluster diagram* (picture) is one way to help you think of ideas to write about. A cluster diagram can help you see how your ideas are connected. In a cluster diagram, you use circles and lines to connect ideas.

A Look at the cluster diagram a student made before she wrote "An Organized Roommate." Notice that she had many ideas about her roommate, but only used the ones that supported her main idea, an organized roommate. Which ideas didn't she use?

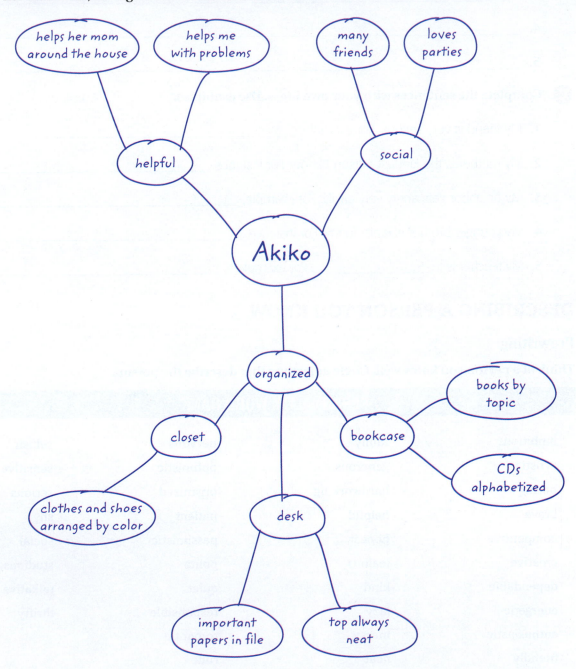

B Now make your own cluster diagram about the person you chose in your prewriting. Write the person's name in the circle. After you make your cluster diagram, you can see which ideas you want to include in your paragraph.

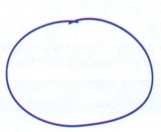

C Write a topic sentence for a paragraph about the **person**. Include the name of the person and an adjective from your cluster diagram.

Topic sentence: _____

D Make a list of several examples that support your topic sentence. Use ideas from your cluster diagram.

1. _____

2. _____

3. _____

✏ Writing

Use your cluster diagram and list to help you write a paragraph. Remember to start with your topic sentence. Try to include two or three examples. Write a title.

_____

_____

_____

_____

_____

_____

🔍 Revising

Ⓐ **Exchange paragraphs with a partner. Read the paragraph your partner wrote. Then use the Revising Checklist to help your partner improve the paragraph.**

REVISING CHECKLIST		
	YES	NO
1. Does the paragraph have a topic sentence?		
2. Does the topic sentence give the name of the person and an adjective that describes him or her?		
3. Are there two or three examples to support the topic?		
4. Is there a title?		
5. Do all of the sentences support the topic?		

Ⓑ **Use your partner's suggestions to revise your paragraph. Write your revised paragraph on a separate piece of paper. Put it in your portfolio.**

ON YOUR OWN

Write a paragraph on one of these topics. Then use the Revising Checklist to improve your paragraph. Give your paragraph a title. Put it in your portfolio.

- Write a paragraph about your own character. Give at least three examples to support your topic sentence. Use the title "More about Me."

- Bring one of your favorite photographs or pictures to class. It can be of someone you know or someone in a magazine. Write a description of the person and share it with your classmates.

- Look at the photograph of Ian on page 107. Write a description of him. Write about what he looks like. Include what he is wearing and what he is doing.

DESCRIBING THINGS

A Work with a partner. Look at the products featured on the Global Gifts website. Write the name of the item under the correct picture.

a. candlesticks

c. flowered plate

e. rectangular rug

b. bath towels

d. leather gloves

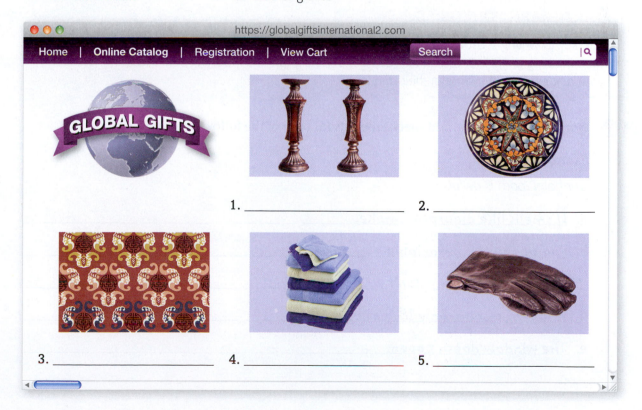

B Read the description of each item. Circle the adjectives.

1. This set of two wooden candlesticks was hand-carved in India. It is a perfect addition to your dining-room table. Each 15-inch candlestick was made from one piece of beautiful Indian rosewood. You can order the set for only $65. (Item 001)

2. This 12-inch round plate was hand-painted in Mexico. The colorful design has pictures of flowers. The bright colors look nice in any room. It is only $40. (Item 002)

3. This rectangular silk and wool rug was made by hand in China. It is 3 feet wide and 6 feet long. The beautiful red and gold geometric pattern is based on Chinese symbols. You can own this beautiful rug for a special price of $530. (Item 003)

4. These plush towels are made of 100% Turkish cotton. You will feel like you're in a spa when you use them. They are so large and soft you can use them at home or at the beach. You can order blue or green. $30 each. (Item 004)

5. These brown leather gloves are made in Brazil and will keep your hands warm in winter. The leather is soft and smooth. You can order a pair of these attractive gloves in size small, medium, or large. Buy them for yourself, or give them as a gift for $35. (Item 005)

PARAGRAPH POINTER: Details

The key to writing a good description is using specific *details.* When you describe what someone or something looks like, you should use lots of details in the supporting sentences. This will help your readers form a picture in their minds.

PRACTICE **A** Work in small groups. Add specific details for each of the following statements.

Example:

Our hotel room is awful.

a. It smells like cigarette smoke.

b. The bed is uncomfortable.

c. The clock and lamp don't work.

d. It is very small—only 18 feet by 20 feet.

e. The window doesn't open.

1. My friend has a nice house.

   a. _____

   b. _____

   c. _____

   d. _____

   e. _____

2. His room is messy.

   a. _____

   b. _____

   c. _____

   d. _____

   e. _____

3. The restaurant is very busy.

   a. _____

   b. _____

   c. _____

   d. _____

   e. _____

4. The building is old and needs repairs.

   a. _____

   b. _____

   c. _____

   d. _____

   e. _____

B **Compare your details with those of another group.**

DESCRIBING A PRODUCT FROM YOUR COUNTRY

Prewriting

Find a picture in a magazine or on the Internet, or draw a picture of a product from your country. Make a list of words and phrases that describe the product. Use words from the word bank.

_____

_____

_____

_____

_____

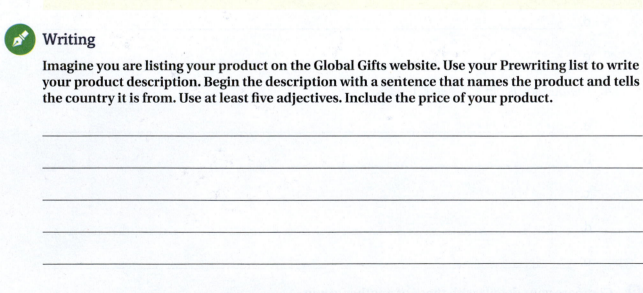

DESCRIPTIVE ADJECTIVE WORD BANK				
Opinion	Shape	Texture	Design	Material
attractive	circular	bumpy	flowered	cotton
beautiful	oval	furry	geometric	gold
bright	rectangular	fuzzy	plaid	leather
interesting	square	rough	plain	plastic
pretty	triangular	smooth	polka-dotted	silk
		soft	solid	silver
			striped	wood
				wool

Writing

Imagine you are listing your product on the Global Gifts website. Use your Prewriting list to write your product description. Begin the description with a sentence that names the product and tells the country it is from. Use at least five adjectives. Include the price of your product.

_____

_____

_____

_____

_____

_____

 **Revising**

A Exchange descriptions and pictures with a partner. Read the description your partner wrote. Then use the Revising Checklist to help your partner improve his or her description.

REVISING CHECKLIST	YES	NO
1. Is the name of the product and the country it is from stated in the first sentence?		
2. Does the description match the picture of the product?		
3. Are there enough details to clearly describe the product?		
4. Are there at least five adjectives in the description?		
5. Is the price given?		

B Use your partner's suggestions to revise your description. Write your revised paragraph on a separate piece of paper. Put the picture and your description of it in your portfolio.

DESCRIBING A GIFT

Prewriting

A You are going to write a description of the best or worst gift you have ever received. Think of a gift and make a cluster diagram that describes it.

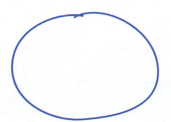

B Answer these questions about the gift.

1. What did you receive? _____

2. Who gave it to you? _____

3. What does it look like? _____

   _____

   _____

4. What color is it? _____

5. What is it made of? _____

6. Why did you receive the gift? Was it a holiday, a birthday, an anniversary, a housewarming

   present? _____

7. Why do (don't) you like it? _____

   _____

C Write a topic sentence for a paragraph about the gift.

   Topic sentence: _____

Writing

Use your cluster diagram and the answers to the questions in Exercise B to help you write a description of the gift. Remember to start with your topic sentence. Include details and adjectives. Write a title.

   _____

   _____

   _____

   _____

   _____

   _____

   _____

   _____

Revising

A Exchange paragraphs with a partner. Read the paragraph your partner wrote. Then use the Revising Checklist to help your partner improve the paragraph.

REVISING CHECKLIST		
	YES	NO
1. Does the paragraph have a topic sentence?		
2. Does the topic sentence say what the gift is and why your partner likes (or doesn't like) it?		
3. Are there enough details to describe the gift?		
4. Are the adjectives used correctly?		
5. Is there a title?		

B Write your revised paragraph on a separate piece of paper. Share your description with your classmates. Put it in your portfolio.

DESCRIBING A CAR

Prewriting

A Look at the pictures of the exterior and interior of a car. With a partner, talk about the parts of a car. Use words from the word bank on page 114.

CAR WORD BANK

accelerator	convertible	hood	rearview mirror	taillight
airbag	cruise control	horn	roof	tire
blinker	dashboard	hubcap	seat	trunk
bucket seat	emergency brake	hybrid	seatbelt	turn signal
bumper	gas tank	license plate	side mirror	wheel
car phone	gear	power brakes	speedometer	windshield
CD player/ radio	GPS navigation	power lock	steering wheel	windshield wiper
clutch	headlight	power window	sunroof	

B Talk to a partner. Describe a car you own, a car you like, or your dream car. Ask and answer these questions.

1. What color is the car?

2. How many doors does it have?

3. What shape and style is it? Is it a hatchback, an SUV, a station wagon, a sports model, a minivan, or a sedan?

4. What kind of seats does it have?

5. How old is it?

6. Does it have a sunroof?

 Writing

A Write five sentences that describe the car.

1. _____

2. _____

3. _____

4. _____

5. _____

B   On a separate piece of paper, write a paragraph describing the car. Begin with a topic sentence. Include details such as color, size, and style. Use at least four adjectives. Add a title.

Revising

A   Exchange paragraphs with a partner. Read the description your partner wrote. Then use the Revising Checklist to help your partner improve the paragraph.

REVISING CHECKLIST	YES	NO
1. Does the paragraph have a topic sentence?		
2. Does the description include details, such as color, size, and style?		
3. Are there enough details to clearly describe the car?		
4. Are there at least four adjectives in the paragraph?		
5. Is there a title?		

B   Write your revised paragraph on a separate piece of paper, and put it in your portfolio.

ON YOUR OWN

Write a paragraph on one of these topics. Then use the Revising Checklist to improve your paragraph. Give your paragraph a title and put it in your portfolio.

- Draw a picture of your national flag. Write about what your flag looks like. Include the colors, shapes, and design. If any of these things have a special meaning, you can write about that, too.

- Describe a piece of sports equipment, such as a tennis racquet, a baseball bat, or a ping-pong paddle.

- Write a description of something that you use every day. For example, you can write about your cell phone or watch.

- What is your favorite painting or piece of art? Describe what it looks like.

- Write a description of your ideal neighbor or roommate.

- Write a description of a character from a movie, TV program, or book.

YOU BE THE EDITOR

The paragraph below has five mistakes with adjectives. With a partner, find and correct the mistakes.

A Birthday Gift

My brother's birthday is next week, and I want to buy him a news sweater. I saw one on the Internet that is made in Canada. I think he will like it. It's a striped sweater blue. My brother has blues eyes, so it will look nice on him. The sweater is made of soft wool, so it is warms. It fits loosely, so it comfortable is to wear. He can wear it to work or on weekends. I'm so happy I had this idea, and I think my brother will be happy, too!

REAL-LIFE WRITING: Completing an Order Form

You want to order something from Global Gifts. Complete this order form.

GLOBAL GIFTS INTERNATIONAL

ORDER TOLL FREE
1-555-555-5555

Send to: _____

Address: _____

_____

City: _____

State: _____ Zip: _____

Country: _____

Item Number	Quantity	Item Description	Color	Gift Wrap	Price	Total Price
				Yes/No		

Payment Method			
Check	Credit Card	Shipping Charge	$6.00
Card Account Number	Expiration ____ / ____ Month Year	**TOTAL**	

Signature _____

REAL-LIFE WRITING: Lost-and-Found Messages

Read the Lost-and-Found messages. Then write your own lost or found message.

LOST AND FOUND

Lost
Our adorable, black, brown, and white beagle—lost near the park. He is 15 inches tall and weighs 22 pounds. His name is Freckles. If you see him, please call or text 555-2421.

Lost
Gold wedding ring lost on Peterson Street. I have had it for 30 years, and it is very important to me. If you find it, please call or text Gabriel at 555-5891.

Found
I found a beautiful, hand-knit red scarf in the cafeteria. Email me at DB@school.edu if you think it is yours.

LOST AND FOUND

_____

_____

_____

_____

_____

_____

_____

....

LEARNING OUTCOMES

Paragraph Writing: Write a paragraph describing a place

Real-Life Writing: Write a friendly letter; address an envelope

DESCRIBING A ROOM

A Look at the picture of a student's bedroom. Then underline the adjectives in the model paragraph "A Cozy Bedroom."

A Cozy Bedroom

My bedroom is small and cozy. There are two big windows on the back wall, so my room is usually bright and sunny. On the left wall, I have a wooden desk with three drawers where I do my homework. All of my books are in a bookcase next to the desk. My bed is against the right wall. There is a painting of a bowl of fruit and flowers above my bed. I love the bright colors of the flowers. I also have a large dresser next to my bed. There are several photographs of my family on top of it and a square mirror above it. Finally, there is a green and white oval rug in front of the dresser. I enjoy spending time in my bedroom because it is so comfortable.

B   Look at the pictures below and on page 120. They show three dormitory rooms. In small groups, discuss each picture and make a list of the things in each room. Use the word bank to help you.

<table>
<tr><td colspan="3" align="center">**ROOM WORD BANK**</td></tr>
<tr><td>alarm clock</td><td>computer / laptop / tablet</td><td>painting</td></tr>
<tr><td>bedspread</td><td>curtains</td><td>picture</td></tr>
<tr><td>blinds</td><td>desk</td><td>pillow</td></tr>
<tr><td>book</td><td>drawer</td><td>plant</td></tr>
<tr><td>bookcase</td><td>dresser</td><td>poster</td></tr>
<tr><td>bulletin board</td><td>fan</td><td>printer</td></tr>
<tr><td>bunk bed</td><td>hockey stick</td><td>rug</td></tr>
<tr><td>camera</td><td>ice skates</td><td>shelf</td></tr>
<tr><td>carpet</td><td>lamp</td><td>stereo</td></tr>
<tr><td>cell phone</td><td>laundry basket</td><td>tennis racquet</td></tr>
<tr><td>chair</td><td>mirror</td><td>TV</td></tr>
<tr><td>closet</td><td>nightstand / bedside table</td><td>wastebasket</td></tr>
</table>

Room 1

_____

_____

_____

_____

_____

_____

_____

_____

Room 2

_____

_____

_____

_____

_____

_____

_____

Room 3

_____

_____

_____

_____

_____

_____

_____

C What adjectives would you use to describe each room? Write words from the word bank, or other words you know.

DESCRIPTION WORD BANK

clean	comfortable	large	neat	small
cluttered	cozy	messy	orderly	sunny

Room 1	Room 2	Room 3
messy		

GRAMMAR FOR WRITING: *There Is* and *There Are*

There is and **There are** are very common phrases in English. We use these phrases at the beginning of a sentence to say that something exists in a specific place. The subject of the sentence comes after the verb *be*.

Examples:

There is *a big window in the classroom.*

There is *one computer in my office.*

There are *lots of windows in the classroom.*

There are *many computers in the library.*

Study the rules for *There is* and *There are*.

RULE	EXAMPLE
Use **There is** with singular noun subjects.	**There is** a dictionary on the table.
Use **There are** with plural noun subjects.	**There are** some books on the table.

PRACTICE

A Underline the sentences with *There is* and *There are* in "A Cozy Bedroom" on page 118.

B Circle *There is* or *There are* to complete each sentence correctly.

1. *There is / There are* lots of books on the bed.

2. *There is / There are* a family photograph on the desk.

3. *There is / There are* a poster on the wall above the bed.

4. *There is / There are* several plants on the windowsill.

5. *There is / There are* a laptop on the table.

6. *There is / There are* a new lamp in the corner of the room

7. *There is / There are* lots of dirty clothes in the laundry basket.

8. *There is / There are* only one window in the bedroom.

C Work with a partner. Write three sentences beginning with *There is* or *There are* for each room on pages 119–120.

Room 1

1. _____

2. _____

3. _____

Room 2

1. _____

2. _____

3. _____

Room 3

1. _____

2. _____

3. _____

GRAMMAR FOR WRITING: Prepositions of Place

When you want to explain where something is located, you can use **prepositions of place**. Prepositions of place help you describe where items are located in relation to other items.

PRACTICE **A** **Look at the pictures. Complete the descriptions with the correct words from the word bank.**

PREPOSITIONS OF PLACE WORD BANK

above	beside	in	in front of	on	on the right
behind	between	in back of	next to	on the left	under

1.

My living room is my favorite room in my house. The blue couch is big and comfortable. There are three pictures _____ the couch. The coffee table is _____ the couch. There are some flowers _____ the vase _____ the coffee table. There's a tall lamp between the couch and the armchair. I love to sit and read or watch TV in the blue and white flowered armchair _____ the couch.

2.

I spend a lot of time working in my office. There are lots
of books _____ the bookcase. The printer is
_____ a table _____ the bookcase
and the desk. There is a laptop _____ the desk.
The wastebasket is _____ the desk. There's a
comfortable black leather chair _____ the desk.
It's the perfect office for getting work done!

B **Look at the picture. Draw the objects in the correct place in the picture. Then compare your picture with a classmate's.**

1. Draw a bowl of fruit in front of the grandmother.

2. Draw a napkin under the table.

3. Draw a cat in front of the fireplace.

4. Draw a clock on the wall behind the grandfather.

5. Draw a vase between the candles on the table.

6. Draw a flower in the vase.

7. Draw a cake next to the coffee cups on the buffet table.

8. Draw a painting on the wall above the buffet table with the cake.

DESCRIBING YOUR CLASSROOM

 Prewriting

Look around your classroom. Complete the chart.

YOUR CLASSROOM	
1. What size is your classroom? Is it big? Small?	
2. What color are the walls?	
3. How many windows are there?	
4. How are the students' desks arranged? Are they in rows? Are they in a circle?	
5. Where does the teacher sit?	
6. Where is the door?	
7. Is there a carpet? If so, what color is it?	
8. What else is in the room (board, clock, posters, computer, whiteboard)? Where are they?	
9. Do you like your classroom? Why or why not?	

Writing

Use the information in the chart to write a paragraph that describes your classroom. Use at least three prepositions of place. Also, write at least one sentence with *There is* and one sentence with *There are*. Remember to begin with your topic sentence and include a title.

_____

_____

_____

_____

_____

_____

_____

 **Revising**

A Exchange paragraphs with a partner. Read the paragraph your partner wrote. Then use the Revising Checklist to help your partner improve the paragraph.

REVISING CHECKLIST		
	YES	NO
1. Does the paragraph begin with a topic sentence?		
2. Does the paragraph have enough details about the classroom?		
3. Does the paragraph include sentences with *There is* and *There are*?		
4. Is there a title?		
5. Are there at least three prepositions of place?		
6. Does the paragraph allow you to "see" the classroom?		

B Use your partner's suggestions to revise your paragraph on a separate piece of paper. Put it in your portfolio.

PARAGRAPH POINTER: Space-Order Paragraphs

When you write a paragraph that describes a place, you arrange the details according to where things are located. This is called *space order*. Use prepositions of place to make the description clear to the reader.

When you organize the details using space order, you should follow a plan. For example, you can describe something from the top to the bottom, from the nearest point to the farthest point, from the right side to the left side, or from the front to the back.

DESCRIBING YOUR FAVORITE ROOM

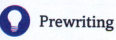 **Prewriting**

A Draw a simple picture of your favorite room. Describe it to a partner.

B Make a list of the things in your favorite room.

_____   _____

_____   _____

_____   _____

_____   _____

Writing

A Answer these questions about your favorite room.

1. What size is the room?

   _____

2. What adjectives would you use to describe it?

   _____

3. What pieces of furniture do you have in your room?

   _____

4. What else is there in your room?

   _____

5. Are there any windows? Is it sunny or dark?

   _____

6. What color are the walls?

   _____

7. Why do you like this room?

   _____

B Complete this sentence for your topic sentence.

   My favorite room in my _____ _is_ _____

C Use the sentences in Exercise A to write a paragraph that describes your room. Use at least three prepositions of place. Also, write at least one sentence with *There is* and one sentence with *There are*. Remember to begin with your topic sentence and include a title.

_____

_____

_____

_____

_____

_____

_____

_____

_____

_____

🔍 Revising

A Exchange paragraphs with a partner. Read the paragraph your partner wrote. Then use the Revising Checklist to help your partner improve the paragraph.

REVISING CHECKLIST		
	YES	NO
1. Does the paragraph begin with a topic sentence?		
2. Does the paragraph have enough details?		
3. Does the paragraph include sentences with *There is* and *There are*?		
4. Are there at least three prepositions of place?		
5. Is there a title?		
6. Does the paragraph allow you to "see" the classroom?		

B Use your partner's suggestions to revise your paragraph. Write your revised paragraph on a separate piece of paper. Put it in your portfolio.

DESCRIBING A PICTURE

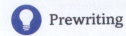

Prewriting

Look at the famous photograph called *Lunchtime atop a Skyscraper*, taken by Charles C. Ebbets in 1932. It shows New York City construction workers eating lunch.

Write four sentences that describe the photograph. Use the present progressive and prepositions of place.

1. _____

2. _____

3. _____

4. _____

Writing

Use the sentences you wrote to write a paragraph describing the picture. Give your paragraph a title. Write it on a separate piece of paper.

Revising

A Exchange paragraphs with a partner. Read the paragraph your partner wrote. Then use the Revising Checklist to help your partner improve the paragraph.

REVISING CHECKLIST		
	YES	NO
1. Does the paragraph begin with a topic sentence?		
2. Does the paragraph have enough details?		
3. Does the paragraph use the present progressive correctly?		
4. Are there at least three prepositions of place?		

B Use your partner's suggestions to revise your paragraph. Write your revised paragraph on a separate piece of paper. Put it in your portfolio.

USE YOUR IMAGINATION

Prewriting

A Imagine you have just moved into a new apartment. This is the living room. It is very simple and plain. The walls are empty and there is very little furniture and no decorations.

Talk to a partner. Use your imagination. Your landlord is going to pay for everything, so don't worry about money! What things would you put in the room? Draw a picture of the room.

B Look at your drawing of the living room. Make a list of the furniture and other items you put in the room.

_____   _____

_____   _____

_____   _____

Writing

Write a description of the living room you drew in Exercise A. Use at least three prepositions of place. Include at least one sentence with *There is* and one sentence with *There are*. Begin with a topic sentence. Include a title.

_____

_____

_____

_____

_____

_____

_____

_____

 **Revising**

A **Exchange paragraphs with a partner. Read the paragraph your partner wrote. Then use the Revising Checklist to help your partner improve the paragraph.**

REVISING CHECKLIST	YES	NO
1. Does the paragraph begin with a topic sentence?		
2. Does the paragraph have enough details about the living room?		
3. Does the paragraph include sentences with *There is* and *There are*?		
4. Are there at least three prepositions of place?		
5. Does the paragraph allow you to "see" the living room?		

B **Use your partner's suggestions to revise your paragraph on a separate piece of paper. Put it in your portfolio.**

ON YOUR OWN

Write a paragraph on one of these topics. Then use the Revising Checklist to improve your paragraph.

- Write a description of an unusual room.
- Write a paragraph describing the nicest or worst hotel room you have stayed in.
- What is your favorite restaurant? Describe what it looks like in a paragraph.
- Write a description of a bus or taxi in your city. What does it look like on the outside? What does it look like on the inside?
- What does your locker at school look like? Is it messy or neat? Write a description of it.
- Write a paragraph describing the closet where you keep your clothes and shoes. How big is it? Does it have any shelves? Is it messy or neat?
- Write a paragraph describing a park in your city or town.

YOU BE THE EDITOR

Read the paragraph. It has seven mistakes with prepositions of place and with *There is* and *There are*. With a partner, find and correct the mistakes.

A Messy Bedroom

My son's bedroom is a mess. He didn't make his bed or hang up his clothes. There is dirty clothes in the floor. I even found dirty clothes between his bed. His schoolbooks and papers are all over his desk. There are an empty soda can of his night table. The top of his dresser is covered with newspapers and magazines. There are a wet towel on the chair instead of at the laundry basket. I wish he would clean up his room!

REAL-LIFE WRITING: Writing Friendly Letters

A friendly letter is a letter you write to a friend or relative. Friendly letters are also called personal letters. Friendly letters are informal. You can use contractions. You can write them by hand or on a computer or tablet or even on your cell phone. Many people these days write informal letters using the Internet, but some people still handwrite letters. It makes the communication very personal.

There are five main parts to a friendly letter. Look at the parts labeled on the letter that a student wrote to her mother.

Date ——
January 2

Greeting ——
Dear Mom,

Body ——
    I just moved into my new apartment. It's on the second floor of a building near school. The thing I like most about the apartment is that it's very sunny. There are big windows in every room. It has a large living room with a fireplace. There are bookcases on two walls. The kitchen is small, but the appliances are new. There is a long hall next to the kitchen that leads to the bedroom and bathroom. There is new carpeting in the bedroom. The only problem is that the closet in the bedroom is very small. I can't wait for you to visit me.

Closing ——
Love,

Name ——
Sema

Study this guide for writing friendly letters.

Rule	Example
1. Include the date	March 23, 2016 or 3/23/2016

2. Begin the greeting with a capital letter (for example, *D* or *H*) and end with a comma (,) after the person's name.	The most common greeting for friendly letters is:
	
	    Dear _____,
	
	Other greetings you can use are:
	
	    Hi, _____.
	
	    Hello, _____.

3. Begin the closing with a capital letter and end it with a comma (,).	Some common closings are:
	
	    Love,
	
	    Your friend,
	
	    Take care,
	
	    Warm regards,
	
	    Best wishes,

Rule	**Example**
4. Use contractions where possible.	Some common contractions are: *I'm* *You're* *It's* *Can't* *We're* *They're* *She's* *Isn't*

Prewriting

A   **You are going to write a letter to a friend who is coming to visit you. First, describe your city or town to a partner.**

B   **Make a cluster diagram of the places to go and things to do in the city where you live. Put the name of your city or town in the center circle.**

 **Writing**

Use your cluster diagram to complete the letter.

_____ (date)

Dear _____ ,

      I was so happy when you called to tell me you were coming to _____ to visit me. There are lots of places to go and things to see and do here. We can _____

_____

_____

_____

_____

_____

_____

_____ ,

_____

Revising

A Exchange your letter with a partner. Read the letter your partner wrote. Then use the Friendly Letter Revising Checklist to help your partner improve the letter.

FRIENDLY LETTER REVISING CHECKLIST	YES	NO
1. Does the letter include the date?		
2. Does the letter have a greeting?		
3. Does the letter have a body?		
4. Does the letter have a closing and signature?		
5. Does the letter use correct punctuation and capitalization?		

B Use your partner's suggestions to revise your letter on a separate piece of paper. Put it in your portfolio.

REAL-LIFE WRITING: Addressing an Envelope

A   Look at the sample envelope.

Toby Boxer
52 Walden Street
Ames, IA 50010

US

Ms. Charlotte Brown
234 Benefit Street
Providence, RI 02912

B   Address the envelope for the letter you wrote to your friend on page 134. Put your name and address in the upper left-hand corner. Then put the person's name and address in the middle.

US

CHAPTER **8** Writing a Narrative

LEARNING OUTCOMES
Paragraph Writing: Write a paragraph about an experience you have had
Real-Life Writing: Write a postcard about your vacation

WRITING A STORY

Read the story. Number the pictures to tell the story in the correct time order.

A Frightening Experience

Last week, I had a frightening experience on an elevator. I was on my way to have dinner at my friend's apartment. I got on the elevator in the lobby and pushed the button for the fifth floor. The elevator stopped at the third floor, and a woman got on with her husband and her baby. The woman pushed the button for the eighth floor. Then the doors closed, and the elevator started to go up. A few seconds later, the elevator stopped suddenly. I felt the elevator bounce up and down two times. We all looked at each other, and the baby began to cry. I was very nervous. A few minutes later the elevator door opened. We were stuck between the third and fourth floors. The third floor was about five feet down. Luckily, I had my cell phone with me, and I called my friend. We waited in the elevator for about ten minutes, but it felt like ten hours. Finally, my friend brought a ladder to the third floor, and we climbed out of the elevator safely. I was happy to be out of the elevator, but my stomach hurt and I couldn't eat dinner.

GRAMMAR FOR WRITING: Simple Past Tense

The *simple past tense* is used to write about events that started and finished in the past.

Study the charts. Notice the forms and rules for the simple past tense.

RULES	EXAMPLES
STATEMENTS Many English verbs are regular and form the simple past by adding *-ed* to the base form of the verb.	I **played** basketball yesterday. You **helped** your brother. She **worked** late. We **watched** TV.
NEGATIVES To write a negative sentence in the simple past, add *did not/didn't* before the base form of the verb.	I **did not (didn't) drive** to school. You **did not (didn't) go** to the movies. He **did not (didn't) bring** his books. They **did not (didn't) watch** the game.
Yes/No **QUESTIONS** To form *yes/no* questions in the simple past use *did* at the beginning of the question. Then add the subject and simple form of the verb.	**Did** you **see** the movie? **Did** he **call** you? **Did** I **miss** the party?
Wh- **QUESTIONS** To form *wh-* questions in the simple past, use the *wh-* question word at the beginning of the question. Then add *did,* and finally add the subject and simple form of the verb.	**What did** you **wear**? **What did** she **read**? **Why did** you **call** me? **Who did** they **invite** for dinner? **Where did** you **go** to high school?

These are the spelling rules for forming the simple past of regular verbs. Study the chart.

VERB ENDING	EXAMPLES
One vowel + *y*: add *-ed* Two consonants: add *-ed* Two vowels + one consonant: add *-ed*	enjoy ➤ enjoy**ed** walk ➤ walk**ed** need ➤ need**ed**
One consonant + *e*: add *-d*	arrive ➤ arrive**d**
One consonant + *y*: change the *y* to *i* and add *-ed*	study ➤ stud**ied**
One vowel + one consonant: double the final consonant and add *-ed*	plan ➤ plan**ned**

The verb *be* forms the simple past tense in a different way. Study the chart.

RULES	EXAMPLES
STATEMENTS The past of *be* has two forms: ***was*** and ***were***. Use ***was*** with *I* and third person singular. Use ***were*** with *you, we* and *they*.	I **was** late for class. We **were** late for class. You **were** late for class. He / She / It **was** late for class. They **were** late for class.
NEGATIVES To form the negative, use ***was not (wasn't)*** or ***were not (weren't)***.	I **was not (wasn't)** late for class. He / She / It **was not (wasn't)** late for class. You **were not (weren't)** late for class. They **were not (weren't)** late for class.
Yes/No* QUESTIONS** To form *yes/no* questions in the simple past of *be*, use ***was/were at the beginning of the question. Then add the subject and simple form of the verb.	**Was** she late for class? **Were** they late for class?
Wh-* QUESTIONS** To form *wh-* questions in the simple past for *be*, use the *wh-* question word at the beginning of the question. Then add ***was/were and finally add the subject and simple form of the verb.	**When were you** at home? **Where was Selim** after class? **Why was she** late for class?

There are also many common irregular verbs in English. Study the chart.

SIMPLE PAST TENSE OF COMMON IRREGULAR VERBS			
Irregular verbs have different forms in simple past statements. They are formed differently than regular verbs. However, questions and negative statements are formed the same as all past tense verbs. *Example:* have Simple past statement: *Yesterday, I **had** a frightening experience.* Question in the past: ***Did** you **have** a bad day? **What kind** of day **did** you **have**?* Negative in the past: *I **didn't have** a very good day.*			
Base Form	**Past Form**	**Base Form**	**Past Form**
beat	beat	have	had
become	became	hurt	hurt
begin	began	leave	left
bring	brought	make	made
build	built	say	said
come	came	see	saw

SIMPLE PAST TENSE OF COMMON IRREGULAR VERBS

drive	drove	sell	sold
fall	fell	speak	spoke
feel	felt	spend	spent
find	found	take	took
fly	flew	teach	taught
get	got	tell	told
give	gave	think	thought
go	went	wake	woke

PRACTICE **A** **Underline the simple past verbs in "A Frightening Experience" on page 136.**

B **Rewrite the paragraph below in the simple past.**

A Busy Day

I have a busy day. I wake up at 7:00 A.M. and get dressed. Then, I eat breakfast, read the paper, and check my email. I send text messages to some of my friends. After that, I take the bus to school and go to classes from 10:00 A.M. to 4:00 P.M. Next, I study for a few hours at the library. At around 5:00 P.M., I have a quick dinner and go to work at the bookstore on campus. At 9:30 P.M., my friend drives me home. When I get home, I watch the news on TV and go to sleep.

_____

I had a busy day yesterday.

_____

_____

_____

_____

_____

_____

_____

C Read "The Google Guys." Fill in the blanks with the correct past form of the verb.

The Google Guys

Sergey Brin and Larry Page _____ (invent)
1.

the Internet search engine Google. Sergey was born in Moscow,

Russia in 1973. His mother and father _____ (be)
2.

both mathematicians. Sergey and his family _____
3.

(not stay) in Russia, They _____ (move)
4.

to the United States when he was six. When Sergey was nine years old, his father

_____ (give) him his first computer. He _____ (love) it, and
5.   6.

from then on, his interest in computers _____ (continue) to grow. Sergey
7.

_____ (graduate) from the University of Maryland in 1993. After that, he
8.

_____ (go) to graduate school at Stanford University.
9.

Larry Page was born in 1973 in Michigan. His father _____ (be) a
10.

professor of computer science, and his mother _____ (teach) computer
11.

programming. Like Sergey, Larry _____ (love) computers at an early age.
12.

Larry _____ (study) computer engineering at the University of Michigan. He
13.

_____ (earn) his B.S.E. (Bachelor of Science in Engineering) in 1995 and
14.

then _____ (go) on to graduate school at Stanford University.
15.

Sergey and Larry _____ (meet) at Stanford and _____
16.   17.

(become) friends. They _____ (write) a paper together and
18.

_____ (create) their own search engine _____ (call)
19.   20.

BackRub. BackRub _____ (grow) in popularity, and in 1998 it
21.

_____ (become) Google.
22.

Google _____ (be) an immediate success. Soon people all over the
23.

world _____ (start) using Google as their search engine. In fact, Google
24.

_____ (make) both men billionaires.
25.

D   Work with a partner. Write five *yes / no* questions about your partner's day yesterday. Then ask your partner the questions and write your partner's answers.

1. Question: _____

   Answer: _____

2. Question: _____

   Answer: _____

3. Question: _____

   Answer: _____

4. Question: _____

   Answer: _____

5. Question: _____

   Answer: _____

E   Now write five *wh-* questions about what your partner did last weekend. Write your questions on a separate piece of paper. Exchange papers and write your answers.

F   Use your questions and answers to write a paragraph about your partner's last weekend.

_____

_____

_____

_____

_____

PARAGRAPH POINTER: Narrative Paragraphs

So far, you have practiced writing several types of paragraphs. You have also learned important things about writing good paragraphs in English. For example, you know that a paragraph has a special form and that it has three parts: a topic sentence, supporting sentences, and a concluding sentence.

In this chapter, you will learn how to write *narrative paragraphs*. A narrative paragraph tells a story about something that happened in the past. When you write a narrative paragraph about the past, you can use the simple past tense and time order to organize your sentences. Also, include time-order signal words. You can review the information about time-order paragraphs and time-order signal words in Chapter 4.

1. Look at the four pictures. They tell a story about a couple who had a bad experience at a restaurant. The pictures are not in the correct order. Number the pictures so they tell the story in a logical order.

2. Write a sentence or two for each picture. Tell what happened. Use the simple past.

Picture 1: _____

_____

Picture 2: _____

_____

Picture 3: _____

_____

Picture 4: _____

3. Take turns telling the story to your partner. Use your sentences.

B   **Each group of sentences tells a story, but the sentences are not in the correct time order. Number the sentences so they follow a logical order. Then use them to write a paragraph.**

1.

_____ My sister called an ambulance, and it took me to the hospital.

_____ On the first day of my visit, I fell down on an icy sidewalk and broke my ankle.

_____ For the rest of my trip, I had to use crutches to get around.

___1___ Last month, I went to Chicago to visit my sister.

_____ After that, I spent five hours at Chicago General Hospital.

My Trip to Chicago

Last month, I went to Chicago to visit my sister.

_____

_____

_____

_____

_____

_____

_____

2.

_____ By lunchtime it was warmer, so I took the sweater off in the cafeteria.

_____ When I told Ellen, she was angry because it was a gift from her boyfriend.

_____ Yesterday, my roommate, Ellen, got very mad at me.

_____ It was cold in the morning, and I borrowed a sweater from her.

_____ After lunch, I forgot about the sweater and left it in the cafeteria.

_____ In fact, Ellen was so angry that she didn't speak to me for the rest of the day.

_____ Later, I went back to get it, but the sweater was gone!

An Angry Roommate

_____

_____

_____

_____

_____

_____

3.

_____ I left school feeling sad because everyone I knew forgot my birthday.

_____ One of my best birthdays was the day I turned eighteen.

_____ Then, I went to school expecting birthday wishes from all of my friends, but not one of my friends or teachers wished me a happy birthday.

_____ I woke up early in a good mood, but when I sat down for breakfast with my family, no one wished me a happy birthday.

_____ It was the best birthday party I ever had.

_____ As soon as I walked in the door, everyone yelled "Surprise! Happy Birthday."

_____ On the way home from school, I noticed that there were a lot of cars parked outside my house, and all the lights were turned off.

_____ I was surprised to see all of my friends and my whole family standing around a big birthday cake.

A Birthday Surprise

_____

_____

_____

_____

_____

_____

_____

4.

_____ The day started off badly when I woke up an hour late and didn't have time to take a shower or eat breakfast.

_____ When I finally got to the office building, the parking lot was full and I had to park two blocks from the building.

_____ My first job interview was a terrible experience.

_____ On my way to the interview, there was a lot of traffic.

_____ I had to walk the two blocks to the office building in the rain without an umbrella.

_____ Obviously, I didn't get the job.

_____ By the time I got to the building, I was an hour late and soaking wet.

_____ When I finally walked into the manager's office, I realized I forgot my résumé.

My Worst Job Interview

_____

_____

_____

_____

_____

WRITING ABOUT A PERSONAL EXPERIENCE

Prewriting

A **Complete the sentences so that each one is true for you.**

1. One of the _____ (happiest / saddest / scariest / most embarrassing)

   memories of my childhood happened when I was _____ years old.

2. A very _____ (funny / embarrassing / surprising) thing happened to me on

   my first day of _____.

3. One summer, my friends and I had a(n) _____ experience.

4. My trip to _____ was very _____.

5. One of the most enjoyable _____ (days / evenings / weeks / weekends) I

   ever spent was _____.

B In small groups, discuss your experiences in Exercise A. Tell what happened in each situation.

C Choose an experience from Exercise A to write a story. List the events you want to write about in your story. Number them in the correct time order. Your story will be a narrative paragraph.

_____   _____

_____   _____

_____   _____

_____   _____

_____   _____

_____   _____

✏️ Writing

Write a story about the experience you chose in the Prewriting. Use the sentence from Exercise A as your topic sentence. Remember to use the simple past tense and time-order signal words. Give your story a title.

_____

_____

_____

_____

_____

_____

_____

Revising

A   Exchange paragraphs with a partner. Read the paragraph your partner wrote. Then use the Revising Checklist to help your partner improve the paragraph.

REVISING CHECKLIST	YES	NO
1. Is there a topic sentence?		
2. Are the sentences in the correct time order?		
3. Are the simple past verbs in the correct form?		
4. Does the paragraph include time-order signal words?		
5. Do all of the sentences relate to the topic?		
6. Is the title written correctly?		

B   Use your partner's suggestions to revise your story on a separate piece of paper. Share your story with your classmates and put it in your portfolio.

USE YOUR IMAGINATION

A   Look at the photo. It shows a traffic jam. A traffic jam is a long line of vehicles that cannot move on a road or can only move very slowly. Talk about the photo with a partner.

B Write a story based on the photo. Imagine that you are in one of the cars. Write about the time and place of your story in the first sentence. Tell what happened in the next few sentences. Use time order to organize your supporting sentences. Use the simple past tense. Include a title.

_____

_____

_____

_____

_____

_____

_____

_____

C Exchange stories with another student. Read your partner's story. Then put your story in your portfolio.

WRITING A BIOGRAPHY OF NEIL ARMSTRONG

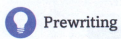 Prewriting

A Look at the photo of astronaut Neil Armstrong. Have you heard of him? In a small group, discuss what you know about him.

B A biography tells the story of a person's life. Look at the timeline of important events in Neil Armstrong's life. Work with a partner. Talk about the important events in Armstrong's life.

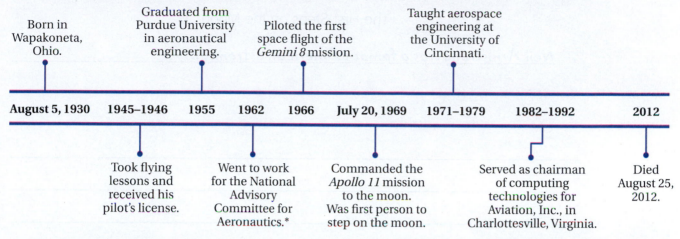

*a government agency that researched airplanes

Writing

A Write at least one complete sentence for each fact on the timeline.

1. _____

2. _____

3. _____

4. _____

5. _____

6. _____

7. _____

8. _____

9. _____

B Look at the sentences you wrote about Neil Armstrong. Add time-order signal words, such as *then, next, after that.*

C Use your sentences to complete the paragraph about Neil Armstrong. Be sure to use time-order signal words so that the order of events is clear. Use simple past tense.

The First Steps on the Moon

<u>Neil Armstrong was a famous American astronaut.</u>

_____

_____

_____

_____

_____

_____

_____

_____

 Revising

A Exchange paragraphs with a partner. Read the paragraph your partner wrote. Then use the Revising Checklist to help your partner improve the paragraph.

REVISING CHECKLIST		
	YES	NO
1. Is there a topic sentence?		
2. Are the sentences in the correct time order?		
3. Are the simple past verbs in the correct form?		
4. Does the paragraph include time-order signal words?		

B Use your partner's suggestions to revise your paragraph. Note: whenever you revise, you can add new information to your paragraph if needed. As you revise your paragraph on Neil Armstrong, add these two sentences to your paragraph and any other information you want to add.

- Armstrong flew more than 200 different models of aircraft, including jets, rockets, helicopters, and gliders.

- His first words after stepping on the moon were, "That's one small step for a man, one giant leap for mankind."

C Write your revised paragraph on a separate piece of paper. Share it with your classmates. Put it in your portfolio.

WRITING A BIOGRAPHY OF CHRISTIANE AMANPOUR

Prewriting

A Look at the photo of Christiane Amanpour. Have you ever seen her on TV? Do you know who she is? Discuss what you know about her in a group.

B Work with a partner. Look at the timeline for Christiane Amanpour. Talk about the important events in her life.

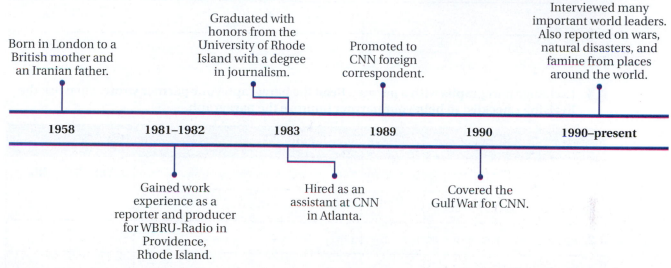

Born in London to a British mother and an Iranian father.

Graduated with honors from the University of Rhode Island with a degree in journalism.

Promoted to CNN foreign correspondent.

Interviewed many important world leaders. Also reported on wars, natural disasters, and famine from places around the world.

1958   **1981–1982**   **1983**   **1989**   **1990**   **1990–present**

Gained work experience as a reporter and producer for WBRU-Radio in Providence, Rhode Island.

Hired as an assistant at CNN in Atlanta.

Covered the Gulf War for CNN.

Writing

A Write at least one sentence for each fact on the timeline. Use a variety of time-order signal words.

1. _____

2. _____

3. _____

4. _____

5. _____

6. _____

7. _____

B Use your sentences to complete the paragraph about Christiane Amanpour. Use the simple past tense where possible.

A Famous Journalist

Christiane Amanpour is one of the most successful international news reporters in the world.

_____

_____

_____

_____

_____

_____

🔍 **Revising**

A Exchange paragraphs with a partner. Read the paragraph your partner wrote. Then use the Revising Checklist to help your partner improve the paragraph.

REVISING CHECKLIST		
	YES	NO
1. Is there a topic sentence?		
2. Are the sentences in the correct time order?		
3. Are the simple past verbs in the correct form?		
4. Does the paragraph include time-order signal words?		

B Use your partner's suggestions to revise your paragraph. Add additional information if needed. Then write your revised paragraph on a separate piece of paper. Put it in your portfolio.

WRITING A BIOGRAPHY OF ICHIRO SUZUKI

Prewriting

A Look at the photo of baseball player Ichiro Suzuki. Discuss what you know about him with a partner.

B Look at the timeline for Ichiro Suzuki. Talk about the important events in Suzuki's life with a partner.

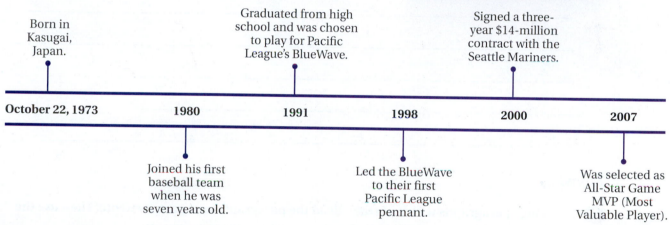

Born in Kasugai, Japan.

Graduated from high school and was chosen to play for Pacific League's BlueWave.

Signed a three-year $14-million contract with the Seattle Mariners.

October 22, 1973   1980   1991   1998   2000   2007

Joined his first baseball team when he was seven years old.

Led the BlueWave to their first Pacific League pennant.

Was selected as All-Star Game MVP (Most Valuable Player).

Writing

A Write at least one sentence for each fact on the timeline. Use time-order signal words.

1. _____

2. _____

3. _____

4. _____

5. _____

6. _____

7. _____

8. _____

B Use your sentences to complete a paragraph about Ichiro Suzuki. Begin with a topic sentence. Add a title.

_____

_____

_____

_____

_____

_____

_____

_____

_____

_____

_____

_____

_____

Revising

A Exchange paragraphs with a partner. Read the paragraph your partner wrote. Then use the Revising Checklist to help your partner improve his or her paragraph.

REVISING CHECKLIST	YES	NO
1. Does the paragraph begin with a topic sentence?		
2. Are the sentences in the correct time order?		
3. Are the simple past verbs in the correct form?		
4. Does the paragraph include time-order signal words?		

B Use your partner's suggestions to revise your paragraph. Write your revised paragraph on a separate piece of paper. Add information if needed. Put it in your portfolio.

WRITING A BIOGRAPHY

Choose one of these two people. Read about the person's life. Or choose another person and do some research about that person. Write a paragraph about the person you choose. Use the simple past tense. Then use the Revising Checklist to improve your paragraph.

Name: GILBERTO GIL

Place of Birth: Salvador, Brazil

Date of Birth: June 29, 1942

Occupation: Musician, songwriter, environmentalist, politician

Accomplishments:
- 1987: Served as Secretary of Culture for the city of Salvador
- 1990: Joined Brazil's Green Party and founded Blue Wave, an environmental protection organization to protect Brazil's waters and coastline
- 2003–2008: Served as Brazilian Minister of Culture
- Released more than 40 albums; had 6 gold records and 4 platinum singles; sold 5 million records

Honors:
- 1998: Grammy Award for Best World Music Album for *Quanta Live*
- 2003: Person of the Year, Latin Academy of Recording Arts and Sciences
- 2005: Grammy Award for Best Contemporary World Music Album for *Eletracústico*

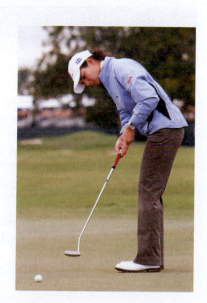

Name: LORENA OCHOA

Place of Birth: Guadalajara, Mexico

Date of Birth: November 15, 1981

Occupation: Professional golfer

Accomplishments:
- Ranked number one female golfer in the world
- 2001: Won the Mexico National Sports Award
- 2003: LPGA (Ladies Professional Golf Association) Rookie of the Year
- 2006, 2007: LPGA Player of the Year
- 2006, 2007, 2008: Vare Trophy (scoring leader)
- 2008: Won the Corona Championship in Mexico; qualified for the World Golf Hall of Fame
- 2010: Retired

WRITING YOUR AUTOBIOGRAPHY

Prewriting

A   Make a timeline of the important events in your own life on a separate piece of paper. Talk about your timeline to a partner.

B   Write at least one sentence for each event on your timeline.

1. _____

2. _____

3. _____

4. _____

5. _____

6. _____

Writing

An autobiography tells the story of your own life. Use your Prewriting sentences to write a paragraph about yourself. Tell where and when you were born in the topic sentence. Use simple past tense and time-order signal words. Write your paragraph on a separate piece of paper.

Revising

A   Exchange paragraphs with a partner. Read the paragraph your partner wrote. Then use the Revising Checklist to help your partner improve the paragraph.

REVISING CHECKLIST		
	YES	NO
1. Is there a topic sentence?		
2. Are the sentences in the correct time order?		
3. Are the simple past verbs in the correct form?		
4. Does the paragraph include time-order signal words?		

B   Use your partner's suggestions to revise your paragraph. Write your revised paragraph on a separate piece of paper. Give it the title "My Autobiography." Put it in your portfolio with your timeline.

USE YOUR IMAGINATION

Using Poetry to Write about Memories

Sometimes it is fun to write a poem about a special memory. Here are some examples of simple *memory poems.*

Lorentza in Monterrey, 4 years old

Sitting in a tree

Waiting for my father to come home from work

Koichi in Tokyo, 11 years old

Playing baseball after school

Eating junk food before dinner

Letizia in Forte dei Marmi, 17 years old

Playing the guitar

Singing with my friends

Abdullah in Jeddah, 8 years old

Riding a donkey

Getting water for my family

A **To write this type of memory poem, think back to a specific time in your childhood. Think about how old you were, where you were, and what you were doing.**

1. On the first line, write your first name and the name of the place where you were.

   _____

2. On the next line, write your age at that time.

   _____

3. On the third line, write exactly what you were doing (use the *-ing* form of the verb).

   _____

4. On the last line, give further information about what was happening (use the *-ing* form of the verb).

   _____

B **Make any changes that you want to make in your memory poem. Copy your memory poem onto a separate piece of paper. Put it in your portfolio with the title "My Memory Poem."**

Memory Drawing

A **Think of a special memory from your childhood. Do a very simple drawing of that memory on a separate piece of paper.**

B **Use the ideas in your drawing to write a paragraph about this memory. Write the revised paragraph under your drawing. When you finish, give it the title "A Memory from My Childhood." Put the drawing and the paragraph in your portfolio.**

ON YOUR OWN

Choose one of the following topics. Write a paragraph about it. Then revise your paragraph to improve it.

- Moving to a new place can be a difficult experience. Write a paragraph about a time you moved.
- Write about a time when you tried to do something but failed.
- Write about an experience that changed the direction of your life.
- Did you ever forget something important? Write about that experience.
- Write about a memorable sporting event in your life.
- Do you remember your first day of school? Write a paragraph about that day.
- Write a paragraph about the life of a famous musician or sports personality you like.

YOU BE THE EDITOR

The paragraph below has six mistakes with simple past verbs. With a partner, find and correct the mistakes.

My First Camping Trip

My first camping trip was not at all what I expected. My brother and I packed our car Friday afternoon and drived five hours to a beautiful campsite in Maine. I thinked it would be hard to put up our tent, but it were easy. It only took a few minutes. We made a fire and cooked a delicious dinner over the fire. We enjoy a beautiful sunset. Then we went into the tent and falled asleep. We were surrounded by the peace and quiet of the trees. There were no bugs and no bears. It rained a little in the night, but we were warm and dry in our tent. When we woked up, the sun was out and we took a walk along the river. What a surprise. I like camping!

REAL-LIFE WRITING

Writing a Postcard

A Read the postcard. It was sent from a student who visited Rio de Janeiro, Brazil. It shows the correct form for writing and addressing a postcard.

Dear Aya,

Rio de Janeiro is awesome! We spent yesterday on Ipanema Beach. Last night we went to some great clubs. Today we went to Carnival, spelled Carnaval in Portuguese. The music, dancing, and costumes were all amazing. Rio is the city that never sleeps, especially during Carnaval! You must visit Rio before you go back to Japan.

See you soon.

Love,

Muriel

Ms. Aya Ochiai

551 West Cedar Street

Ann Arbor, MI 48105

B Draw a simple picture that shows a place you have visited. Then write a message to a friend or relative about your trip. Address the postcard correctly.

Paragraph Writing: Write an opinion paragraph

Real-Life Writing: Write a letter to the editor

WHAT DO YOU THINK?

A Look at the pictures. Write the word or phrase that goes with each picture. Use words from the word bank.

PUBLIC PLACES WORD BANK				
airport	hotel room	park	shopping mall	taxi
auditorium	movie theater	restaurant	stadium	train
bus stop	office			

1. _____

2. _____

3. _____

4. _____

5. _____

6. _____

7. _____   8. _____   9. _____

10. _____   11. _____   12. _____

B Many cities have laws that do not allow smoking in public places. What's your opinion? Talk to a partner about where you think smoking should not be allowed. Draw the "No Smoking" sign below the places in Exercise A.

C Read the model paragraphs, and write the answers to the questions.

1.

No Smoking in Public Places

I think smoking should be illegal in public places. Most importantly, nonsmokers have a right to clean air. They should not have to be around cigarette smoke. Like most nonsmokers, I hate it when my clothes smell like cigarette smoke. It is disgusting, and it is also dangerous. Another reason smoking should not be allowed in public places is that it is so bad for the health of smokers. People can get sick and even die from breathing second-hand smoke. Finally, I believe that a law making smoking illegal in public places will help smokers quit smoking. If smokers do not quit because of the cost or the dangers to their health, maybe these new laws will help them quit.

a. What is the author's opinion?

_____

b. What reasons does the author give to support this opinion?

_____

_____

_____

_____

c. Where does the author put the most reason to support this opinion?

_____

2.

Smokers Have Rights

It is unfair to make smoking illegal in public places. For one thing, nonsmokers should not have more rights than smokers. Also, if nonsmokers don't want to be in a smoke-filled room, they can go somewhere else. In addition, smoking is a legal activity. I do not believe that the government should tell people that a legal activity is illegal in some places. Most importantly, I think prohibiting smoking in places like restaurants is bad for business. Maybe both smokers and nonsmokers should try to be a little more understanding.

a. What is the author's opinion?

_____

b. What reasons does the author give to support this opinion?

_____

_____

_____

_____

c. Where does the author put the most reason to support this opinion?

_____

GRAMMAR FOR WRITING: *Should*

We often use *should* or *should not* (*shouldn't*) to give an opinion or advice.

Study the charts. Notice the form and the rules for using *should*.

STATEMENTS	I think we **should** take the English course.
	He **should** exercise every day.
	You **should** eat a healthy breakfast.
	You **should** turn off the lights when you leave a room.
NEGATIVE STATEMENTS	People **should not (shouldn't)** talk on their cell phones in restaurants.
	We **should not (shouldn't)** drive cars that use a lot of gas.
	You **should not (shouldn't)** leave the window open.
QUESTIONS	**Should** I email Tom about the meeting?
	Should they take driving classes?
	Should she get a part-time job?
	When **should** we leave?
	Who **should** I call?
	Where **should** they study?

RULE	EXAMPLE
Always use the base form of the main verb after ***should***.	Maria **should** sign the lease immediately. (CORRECT)
	Maria **should** ~~signed~~ the lease immediately. (INCORRECT)
Do not add *-s* to ***should*** even if you are using the third person singular.	My brother **should** work harder. (CORRECT)
	My brother ~~**shoulds**~~ work harder. (INCORRECT)
Do not use an infinitive (***to*** + base form) after ***should***.	You **should** stop smoking. (CORRECT)
	You **should** ~~to stop~~ smoking. (INCORRECT)

PRACTICE **A** **Complete the sentences with *should* or *shouldn't*.**

1. That music is too loud. Our neighbors _____ play music that loud at night.

2. If your tooth still hurts tomorrow, you _____ go to the dentist.

3. The movie starts at 3:00 so we _____ leave for the theater by 2:30. It takes about half an hour to get there.

4. Before you go to Turkey for your vacation, you _____ learn some Turkish. You will enjoy your trip a lot more.

5. It's supposed to rain this afternoon. You _____ take an umbrella.

6. They have a big exam tomorrow. They _____ go to the movies tonight. They _____ stay home and study.

7. Jerry has a headache. He _____ take an aspirin.

8. Evelyn _____ ask Mohammed to help her with her homework. He took the same course last semester.

9. Jessica wants to lose weight. She _____ do some exercise.

10. Justin is always tired in the morning. He _____ stay up so late at night.

B **Read the sentences. Correct the mistakes. One sentence is correct. Circle it.**

1. Hassan should made dinner for his friends.

2. My sister shoulds quit smoking.

3. You should to drive carefully on icy roads.

4. We should took a taxi.

5. Kim should go to the doctor.

6. He shouldn't to talk on his cell phone during the movie.

C **Write two sentences of advice for each situation. Use *should* in one sentence and *shouldn't* in the other.**

1. Sarah has a toothache.

a. _She should go to the dentist._

b. _She shouldn't eat candy._

2. Karen burned her hand.

a. _____

b. _____

3. Emma has a cold.

a. _____

b. _____

4. Paula has the hiccups.

a. _____

b. _____

5. Jim has a fever.

a. _____

b. _____

6. Stan has a stomachache.

a. _____

b. _____

D Compare your sentences with a partner's. Did you give the same advice?

ORDER OF IMPORTANCE

PARAGRAPH POINTER: Order of Importance Paragraphs

You have learned to organize the supporting sentences in paragraphs according to time and space order. Now you will practice organizing supporting sentences by listing them according to their *order of importance*.

When you use order of importance, you list your ideas from most important to least important or least important to most important. If you think all of your ideas are equally important, the order does not matter. When you write your paragraph, use signal words to help the reader understand your ideas.

Before you write a paragraph that expresses your opinion, you should make a list of reasons to support your opinion. Then, you should arrange the reasons according to their order of importance.

ORDER OF IMPORTANCE SIGNAL WORDS BANK

also,	first of all,	in addition,	moreover,	secondly,
finally,	for one thing,	last of all,	most importantly,	

PRACTICE **A** **Read the paragraphs. Circle the signal words. Which paragraph begins with the author's most important point? Which paragraph ends with the author's most important point?**

1.

Restricting Cell Phone Use

I think there should be a ban on using cell phones in most public places, in forms of public transportation, and while driving. For one thing, I have to listen to other people's conversations. I also have to listen to the sound of cell phones ringing while I'm trying to watch a movie, read a book in the library, or listen to a concert. Moreover, the use of cell phones in religious places like churches or mosques is disrespectful. Most importantly, people should not be allowed to talk on their cell phones while they are driving. These people risk having an accident and hurting themselves, their passengers, and other drivers. I believe laws need to be passed to limit or ban the use of cell phones in certain places.

2.

Freedom to Talk

In my opinion, it is unfair to ban cell phones in public places and in forms of transportation, including automobiles. Most importantly, people have a legal right to use their cell phones since they are paying for the service. Most people remember to turn off their phones during movies and concerts and while they are in museums and libraries anyway. Secondly, many businesspeople would be seriously affected by a ban since they spend a lot of time traveling and communicating with their clients on cell phones. They need to work while they are on planes or trains or even while they are driving. Finally, cell phones are essential in emergency situations.

B Complete the opinion paragraphs below with signal words and phrases from the word bank.

1.

My Cell Phone

The most valuable invention in my lifetime is the cell phone. _____, my cell phone keeps me connected to my friends and family no matter where I am. Even if someone is in another country, it's easy to make long-distance calls with a cell phone. _____, my cell phone can do lots of other things besides making calls. For instance, I can send text messages, browse the Internet, take pictures and videos, read books, listen to music, get directions, and play games. _____, I feel safer with my cell phone. For example, I can use it in an emergency if my car breaks down or I get lost. My cell phone is small in size, but it is a big help to me.

2.

Traveling by Bicycle

Riding a bicycle is a smart way to travel. _____, riding a bike is much cheaper than driving a car because you never have to buy gas. _____, riding a bike is a great way to exercise and stay in shape. _____, riding a bicycle is much better for the environment than driving a car or taking a bus because bikes do not create any pollution. As you can see, there are many advantages to riding a bike, no matter where you live.

WRITING ABOUT YOUR OPINIONS

Prewriting

A Write your opinion by completing the sentences with *should* or *should not*. Then share your opinions with a partner.

1. Police officers _____ carry a gun.

2. All students _____ learn a second language.

3. It _____ be illegal for people to use cell phones while they are driving.

4. Animals _____ be used in scientific research.

5. Companies _____ make people retire when they are sixty-five years old.

6. Parents _____ limit the amount of time their children spend on the Internet.

7. Students _____ take a year off between high school and college.

8. Teachers _____ give homework on the weekends.

9. High schools _____ require students to wear uniforms.

10. Colleges and universities _____ offer all courses online.

B **Choose three of the opinions you wrote in Exercise A and give two or three reasons to support each one.**

Opinion 1:

_____

Reason 1:

_____

Reason 2:

_____

Reason 3:

_____

Opinion 2:

_____

Reason 1:

_____

Reason 2:

_____

Reason 3:

_____

Opinion 3: _____

_____

Reason 1: _____

_____

Reason 2: _____

_____

Reason 3: _____

_____

Writing

Choose one of your opinions in the Prewriting as the topic sentence for an opinion paragraph. Then use your reasons to write supporting sentences. Organize your reasons from least important to most important. If all your reasons are equally important, the order does not matter. Remember to use signal words. Give your paragraph a title.

_____

_____

_____

_____

_____

_____

_____

_____

_____

_____

_____

_____

Revising

A Exchange paragraphs with a partner. Read the paragraph your partner wrote. Then use the Revising Checklist to help your partner improve the paragraph.

REVISING CHECKLIST		
	YES	NO
1. Does the topic sentence state the author's opinion?		
2. Are there at least three reasons to support the opinion?		
3. Are the reasons organized according to order of importance? Or are they equally important?		
4. Does the paragraph include signal words?		
5. Is there a title?		
6. Is *should* used correctly?		

B Use your partner's suggestions to revise your paragraph. Write your revised paragraph on a separate piece of paper. Put it in your portfolio.

WRITING ABOUT LEARNING ENGLISH

Prewriting

A Work with a small group. Talk about helpful hints for learning English. Make a list of six things people should and should not do when they are learning English. Write complete sentences using *should* or *should not*.

1. _____

2. _____

3. _____

4. _____

5. _____

6. _____

B Compare your list with another group's. Did you have any of the same ideas?

C Discuss your ideas with the whole class. Add any other ideas you can think of about learning English.

1. _____

2. _____

3. _____

Writing

Write a paragraph giving advice about learning English. Begin with a topic sentence. Use some of the ideas from your Prewriting list as supporting sentences. Give at least three reasons for your opinion. Organize your sentences by order of importance and include signal words. End your paragraph with a concluding sentence. Remember to add a title.

_____

_____

_____

_____

_____

_____

_____

_____

_____

Revising

A Exchange paragraphs with a partner. Read the paragraph your partner wrote. Then use the Revising Checklist to help your partner improve the paragraph.

REVISING CHECKLIST		
	YES	NO
1. Does the topic sentence state the author's opinion?		
2. Are there at least three reasons to support the opinion?		
3. Is there a concluding sentence?		
4. Does the paragraph include signal words?		
5. Is there a title?		
6. Are the sentences organized according to order of importance? Or are they listed as equally important?		

B Use your partner's suggestions to revise your paragraph. Write your revised paragraph on a separate piece of paper. Put it in your portfolio.

WRITING ABOUT INVENTIONS

Prewriting

A Throughout history, people have invented new things to make life better, easier, and safer. Look at the pictures. Write the name of each invention under the correct picture. Use words from the word bank.

INVENTIONS WORD BANK		
airplane	light bulb	telephone
car	penicillin	telescope
computer	printing press	TV

1. _____   2. _____   3. _____

4. _____

5. _____

6. _____

7. _____

8. _____

9. _____

B **Discuss these questions in small groups.**

1. Which three inventions do you think had the biggest effects on society? Why?

2. How do these inventions help people?

3. How do you think these inventions changed the way people live?

4. What other inventions do you think had a big effect on our lives? Make a list.

_____

_____

_____

_____

_____

_____

C Work with a group of classmates. Which invention do you think has had the greatest effect on society? Write your name and opinion in the chart. Then ask the opinion of the people in your group. Complete the chart with their opinions.

NAME	MOST IMPORTANT INVENTION

D Think of three reasons why you chose the invention in Exercise C. Write your opinion and the three reasons on the lines.

Opinion: _____

Reason 1: _____

_____

_____

Reason 2: _____

_____

_____

Reason 3: _____

_____

_____

 **Writing**

Write a paragraph about the invention you think has had the biggest impact on society. Support your opinion with at least three reasons. Remember to organize your paragraph according to order of importance, and use signal words. Give your paragraph a title.

_____

_____

_____

_____

_____

_____

_____

_____

_____

Revising

A Exchange paragraphs with a partner. Read the paragraph your partner wrote. Then use the Revising Checklist to help your partner improve the paragraph.

REVISING CHECKLIST		
	YES	NO
1. Does the topic sentence state the author's opinion?		
2. Are there at least three reasons to support the opinion?		
3. Are the sentences organized according to order of importance? Are the supporting sentences organized using listing order?		
4. Does the paragraph include signal words?		
5. Is there a title?		
6. Do all of the sentences relate to the topic?		

B Use your partner's suggestions to revise your paragraph. Write your revised paragraph on a separate piece of paper. Put it in your portfolio.

USE YOUR IMAGINATION

A Read the letter to The Adviser. Then read The Adviser's response. Discuss the situation and the response with a partner.

Dear Adviser

Dear Adviser,

Earlier this year, my best friend needed to borrow money to buy new tires for his car. I loaned him some money and was glad to help. He promised me that he would pay me back. It has been several months and he has not returned the money. But recently I was at his house. I noticed that he has a new outdoor grill. I want to ask him for the money. I would rather send him a text or email than ask him face to face. What do you think? Should I also ask him about the new grill?

Please advise me!

Thank you,

Unhappy

Dear Unhappy,

A good friendship is based on open communication. I think you can and should talk to your friend face to face. If the time you set for repaying the money is past, or if you did not talk about a timeline, do it now. Don't let it ruin your friendship. Do not assume that your friend bought the grill. Maybe it was a gift.

Good luck!

Sincerely,

The Adviser

B Write your own letter to The Adviser.

Dear Adviser,

_____

_____

_____

_____

_____

_____

_____

_____

_____

_____

C Exchange letters with a partner. Write a response to your partner's letter.

Dear _____ ,

_____

_____

_____

_____

_____

_____

_____

_____

Sincerely,

The Adviser

D Read and discuss the responses you and your partner wrote to each other's letters.

ON YOUR OWN

Write a paragraph supporting one of these opinions. State your opinion in the topic sentence and then support it with several specific reasons or examples. Remember to organize your paragraph according to order of importance and to use signal words. Then use the Revising Checklist on page 176 to improve it.

- Hotels shouldn't allow pets.
- People turning sixty-five should have to retake the driver's test to keep their license.
- Television commercials should be eliminated because they have a bad affect on children.
- All schools should always be single sex, that is only girls or only boys. Girls and boys should not be in the same school.
- There are several advantages (or disadvantages) of using credit cards.
- Living in the country is better than living in the city.
- Living in the city is better than living in the country.
- Students should be required to spend a certain amount of time doing volunteer work in order to graduate.

YOU BE THE EDITOR

The paragraph below has four mistakes with *should*. With a partner, find and correct the mistakes.

Reading to Young Children

Parents should to read to their young children every day. First of all, reading to young children is important because it is an excellent way to bond with them. In addition, young children whose parents read to them have better language skills when they start school. Parents should spending time talking about the stories and pictures. A parent shoulds also explain the meanings of new words. Most importantly, these children often develop a love for reading as they grow older. These are only a few of the reasons that parents no should think reading to young children is a waste of time.

REAL-LIFE WRITING: Writing a Letter to the Editor

A Read the letter to the editor in today's newspaper about teaching art to children.

LETTERS TO THE EDITOR

Dear Editor:

Last week the Board of Education voted to eliminate art classes from our schools. I don't think the Board understands the importance of art. The Board is right in saying that math, science, history, etc., are important for children to learn. It is also right in saying that sports are important for kids' health. The Board is wrong, however, to ignore the creative side of children. People need art. Art helps us express ourselves.

Before Board members make a decision about the education of children, they should educate themselves about the importance of art in our lives. The purpose of our schools is to educate. Is a child educated if he or she doesn't know how to draw? The purpose of education is to help children become well-rounded adults. Art is a subject worth studying.

Yours truly,
A Reader

B Do you agree with the letter? Why or why not? Write a letter to the editor expressing your own opinion about teaching art in school.

LETTERS TO THE EDITOR

Dear Editor:

_____

_____

_____

_____

_____

_____

Yours truly,

A Reader

You Be the Editor
Answer Key

Chapter 1, page 14

A Lucky and Happy Man

My name is Stanley ~~s~~toico. I am ninety years old. I am from ~~i~~taly. I moved to San Diego, ~~c~~alifornia,
with my family when I was nine years old. I speak ~~i~~talian and ~~e~~nglish. ~~i~~n my younger years, I had
many different jobs. I worked hard and saved my money. In 1985, I started my own business. ~~T~~he
business was successful, and ~~i~~ retired in 2008. I like to travel and play golf. I have seen and done a
lot in my long life. I am a lucky and happy man.

Handwritten corrections: S (stoico→Stoico), I (italy→Italy), C (california→California), I (italian→Italian), E (english→English), I (in→In), T (The), I (i→I)

Chapter 2, page 32

My Cousin

My cousin's name is Bettina Lee. She is thirty-seven years old. She was born in Chicago, Illinois,
but now ~~her~~ *she* lives in Denver, Colorado. She is married and has two children. Bettina and ~~me~~ *I* enjoy
spending time together. ~~Us~~ *We* love to go ice-skating. Bettina is an excellent ice-skater. She skated in
ice shows when ~~he~~ *she* was young. Now, Bettina teaches ice-skating to young children. She enjoys
watching ~~their~~ *them*.

Chapter 3, page 53

A Tired New Mother

     I am a proud, but tired mother of twin baby boys. I don't ~~has~~ *have* any free time these days. My days ~~am~~ *are* very busy, and my nights are busy, too. I never ~~gets~~ *get* much sleep anymore. I wake up several times during the night to feed the babies. They ~~have~~ *are* always hungry! So, I am tired in the morning. I try to take naps when the babies are napping, but I have so much to do. I wash baby clothes and blankets every morning and evening. I also ~~changes~~ *change* diapers all day long. Sometimes when both babies ~~cries~~ *cry* at the same time, I cry, too. But when I ~~watches~~ *watch* them sleeping peacefully, I know how lucky I am to have two happy, healthy babies.

Chapter 4, page 69

A Delicious Drink

     Turkish coffee is not easy to make, but it is delicious. There are several ~~way~~ *ways* to make Turkish coffee, but this is the way my friend taught me. First, you will need a special pot called a cezve. Pour 3 ~~cup~~ *cups* of cold water into the pot. Then, add 3 teaspoons of coffee and 3 teaspoons of ~~sugars~~ *sugar* to the water. Next, heat the ~~waters~~ *water* on a low flame until you can see foam forming on top. Don't let it boil. Then, take the pot off the heat. Gently stir the mixture and return it to the heat. Repeat this two more ~~time~~ *times*. Finally, pour the ~~coffees~~ *coffee* into 3 cups. Make sure each person gets some foam, and enjoy your coffee.

Chapter 5, page 90

A Busy Pharmacist and Mother

I am a pharmacist and a mother, and my days are busy. As a pharmacist, my job is to prepare and

sell medicines. Every morning, I get up ~~on~~ *at* 6:30 a.m. I have breakfast with my family and make lunch

for my daughter to take to school. I leave the house at 8:00 a.m. and drive to the drugstore where

I work ~~for~~ *from* 9:00 a.m. ~~at~~ *to* 5:00 p.m. During the day, I fill prescriptions for customers. Sometimes the

customers have questions about their medicines. I answer their questions. I also give them information

about how often to take the medicine. After work, I drive home and have dinner with my family. Then

I help my daughter with her homework ~~during~~ *for* a few hours. Sometimes I read or watch TV ~~at~~ *in* the

evening before I go to bed. I am very busy, but I really enjoy being a pharmacist and a mother.

Chapter 6, page 116

A Birthday Gift

My brother's birthday is next week, and I want to buy him a ~~news~~ *new* sweater. I saw one on the

Internet that is made in Canada. I think he will like it. It's a striped (blue) sweater. My brother has ~~blues~~ *blue*

eyes, so it will look nice on him. The sweater is made of soft wool, so it is ~~warms~~ *warm*. It fits loosely, so it

(comfortable) is to wear. He can wear it to work or on weekends. I'm so happy I had this idea, and I

think my brother will be happy, too!

Chapter 7, page 132

A Messy Bedroom

My son's bedroom is a mess. He didn't make his bed or hang up his clothes. There ~~is~~ *are* dirty

clothes ~~in~~ *on* the floor. I even found dirty clothes ~~between~~ *under* his bed. His schoolbooks and papers are all

over his desk. There ~~are~~ *is* an empty soda can ~~of~~ *on* his night table. The top of his dresser is covered with

newspapers and magazines. There ~~are~~ *is* a wet towel on the chair instead of ~~at~~ *in* the laundry basket. I wish

he would clean up his room!

Chapter 8, page 158

My First Camping Trip

My first camping trip was not at all what I expected. My brother and I packed our car Friday
drove *thought*
afternoon and ~~drived~~ five hours to a beautiful campsite in Maine. I ~~thinked~~ it would be hard to put up
was
our tent, but it ~~were~~ easy. It only took a few minutes. We made a fire and cooked a delicious dinner
enjoyed *fell*
over the fire. We ~~enjoy~~ a beautiful sunset. Then we went into the tent and ~~falled~~ asleep. We were

surrounded by the peace and quiet of the trees. There were no bugs and no bears. It rained a little in
woke
the night, but we were warm and dry in our tent. When we ~~woked~~ up, the sun was out and we took a

walk along the river. What a surprise! I like camping!

Chapter 9, page 179

Reading to Young Children

should read
Parents should ~~to~~ read to their young children every day. First of all, reading to young children is

important because it is an excellent way to bond with them. In addition, young children whose parents
spend
read to them have better language skills when they start school. Parents should ~~spending~~ time talking
should
about the stories and pictures. A parent ~~shoulds~~ also explain the meanings of new words. Most

importantly, these children often develop a love for reading as they grow older. These are only a few of
should not
the reasons that parents (no) should think reading to young children is a waste of time.